poemcrazy

poem

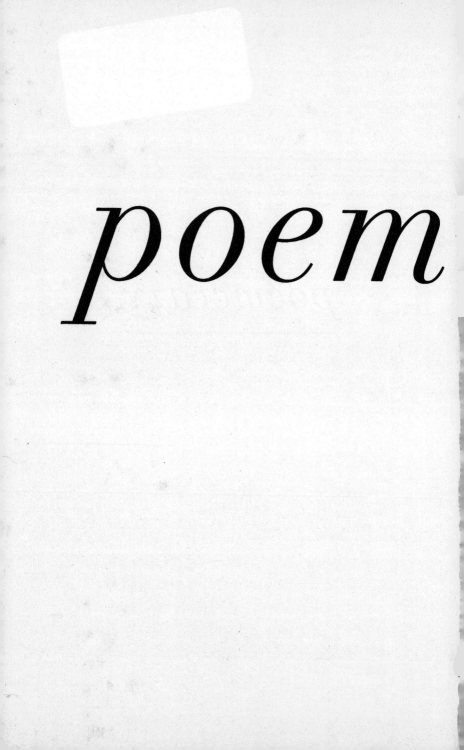

crazy

FREEING YOUR LIFE WITH WORDS

Susan Goldsmith Wooldridge

THREE RIVERS PRESS • NEW YORK

A complete list of credits appears on pages 209-10.

Published by Three Rivers Press, New York, New York.
Member of the Crown Publishing Group.

Random House, Inc. New York, Toronto, London, Sydney, Auckland

www.randomhouse.com

Originally published in hardcover by Clarkson Potter/Publishers in 1996.
First paperback edition published in 1997.

Printed in the United States of America

Book design by Barbara de Wilde

Library of Congress Cataloging-in-Publication Data
Wooldridge, Susan Goldsmith
poemcrazy: freeing your life with words / by Susan Goldsmith Wooldridge.—1st ed.
1. Poetry—Authorship. I. Title
PN1059.A9W66 1996
808.1—dc20 96-2109

ISBN 0-609-80098-1

20 19

For my children, Daniel and Elisabeth,
and for my teacher Jack Mabie, wherever you are

CONTENTS

CONTENTS

5

LIGHTS AND MYSTERIES

I want to thank

Ethel and Julian Goldsmith for providing freedom and a house full of books, talk, art, science, love and support.

My children, Daniel and Elisabeth, for their exciting use of language since they began to speak, inspiring me to catch their words.

Kent Wooldridge for loving literature and coaching me for hours with various word processors.

My friend and writing partner Elizabeth Singh, who's been meeting with me weekly for years—editing, critiquing, meditating, crying, laughing—and keeping me going.

My friend and writing consultant Jane Staw, truly my collaborator, who understood before I did what this book could be, coaxed many chapters and personal stories out of me, helped me focus them and shape the whole.

My marvelous agent, Arielle Eckstut, a multi-gifted dynamo who believed in *poemcrazy* from the start, helped put the book in its present form and found the perfect editor/publisher for me.

My editor/publisher, Carol Southern, who regularly delights me with her brilliance, vision, integrity, patience and ear.

Associate editor Eliza Scott, production editor Mark McCauslin and others from Clarkson Potter and Crown who have helped with the book along the way—including Deanne Adlen-Chalk, Kate Fay, Jane Treuhaft, Marcia Purcell, Margot Schupf, Gail Shanks, and Amy Zelvin.

My friends and cohorts Joanne Allred, Nancy Berg, Martha Bergland, Duane BigEagle, Kevin Cahill, Tom Centolella, Anthony Cuellar, Liz Dulany, Kathleen Gallo, Annie Gottlieb, Jack Grapes, Jane

Hirshfield, Barbara Jennings, Jim Karman, Tanha Luvaas, Sharon Paquin, Wayne Pease, Chris Reynolds, Heather Riddel, Andrea Ross, Thomasin Saxe, Dave Schleiger, Beth Spencer, Susan Terence and Alice Worsley, whose support and suggestions have been invaluable.

Ron Padgett, for seeing the potential in a rambling first draft.

My friends Ed Steinbrecher and Stephen Connors, who developed and teach inner guide meditation.

The California Poets in the Schools organization (CPITS), for having the spunk and vision to thrive against all odds—bringing practicing poets into classrooms since 1964. This book was inspired by my work in CPITS. Ideas similar to those in many of the practice pages are used by my CPITS colleagues. I'm grateful to all who have helped generate them.

The scores of children and teachers who've worked with me for fifteen years, along with all the adults in workshops who have made me believe again and again in the magic of poetry.

Many more people—some appear in these pages—who have helped me in ways too numerous to mention. You know who you are.

. . . Poetry arrived
in search of me. I don't know, I don't know where
it came from, from winter or a river.
I don't know how or when. . . .
—Pablo Neruda

ORDINARY MAGIC

Poems arrive. They hide in feelings and images, in weeds and delivery vans, daring us to notice and give them form with our words. They take us to an invisible world where light and dark, inside and outside meet.

I've been playing with words and shaping poems in the pages of my journal since I was fourteen. Often it seems I just catch my heart and mind's dictation and take notes. Other times I let a ginkgo tree, a pearl ring, a sign along the highway speak to me. I've learned that in a safe, free setting anyone of any age can gather words, play with language and write poems, sometimes with what poet Anne Waldman calls "goofy profundity."

It's impossible to *teach* anyone to write a poem. But we can set up circumstances in which poems are likely to happen. We can create a field in and around us that's fertile territory for poems. Playing with words, we can get to the place where poems come from. We can write and make discoveries about who we are and who we might become whether or not we truly commit ourselves to becoming poets.

In these chapters I introduce my world and tell you stories about my life with words. I also include poems written in workshops by people of all ages. In numerous practices I invite you to drop a line into the pool of words around you and within you to begin making poems that express more than words can say, an act Allen Ginsberg calls "ordinary magic."

—Susan Goldsmith Wooldridge
Chico, California, November 1995

1

Following words

1

outlaw on a poem walk

We walked through night 'til night was a poem.
—Brenda Hillman

I like to begin walks on the bridge at One Mile. There's always action here in the park near my house a mile from downtown Chico. Water rushes over the dam. Trout and trout shadows dart about the still spots. In summer there's a sweet, creek, sycamore smell.

Today it's early September and oak galls are dropping—the puffy golf-sized balls oak trees form around wasp larvae. A blackened gall spins on a step of the dam below the bridge. The gall bobs under the tiny falls and hops back up in a circle like a science class experiment nobody's watching but me.

I've met Ethiopians here, Italians, Pomo natives and the design director of a made-for-TV movie walking with her dog, Moo Moo. Once a legless veteran raced his wheelchair down the ramp into the middle of the creek, where he played wailing blues harmonica. On another walk I watched a cluster of Hmong women gather green creek moss in baskets.

For me, poetry is related to walking. Words and images fill me when I wander somewhere alone. Writer Bruce Chatwin lived with nomads and believed inspiration, as well as true rest, could best be found in motion. Sometimes I wish I could walk forever, jotting down notes and words. And the bridge at One Mile is a perfect spot to begin.

Poems don't normally have much to do with intention for me. They're more likely to come unexpectedly in a place like this. Since it's past Labor Day the dam is slanted low and the park's huge swimming pool is shallow. Upstream a small girl wades with her mother. The mom's red shirt is reflected like a scarlet lily pad floating in front of her. The two waddle in deeper, wetting their clothes. Now the mother swirls her girl through the water as if she were a minnow on a fishing line.

Here's a damsel fly, electric blue. Images for poems flit about and I've barely begun to walk. An elderly man and woman lean over the bridge. They're each wearing an orange, pink and turquoise shirt covered with race cars and the words WILD CHILD in bold black on the back. The man sports a cap labeled OUTLAW, as if defining the unruly part in each of us that's a poet.

Poems hang out where life is. Often I see outlaw kids careen with their bikes over the pool's edge into the creek, where they pedal-swim-slog through water. I've just said *Hi* to a boy and his toddler brother, who babbles to me. The older brother warns, "Don't talk to strangers." Especially outlaw strangers like me, writing it all down.

Farther up creek I spot a patch of mint that goes into my notebook in words and fragrant clumps I stuff between the pages. I find figs, wild grapes, blackberries on these nourishing, edible walks.

Here's the old campfire circle where, the first summer of Shakespeare in the Park, Romeo died at my children's feet. "Laws of the Campfire" are set in the cement like Boy Scout badges. I've been here dozens of times and never noticed these messages before in colorful, tile chips at my toes—*Seek beauty. Give service. Be happy. Bluebirds. Wood gatherer, Torch Leader, Fire maker*... The final, mysterious tile says *Ki Ku Wa Ya.* On this poem walk I feel ready for anything to happen or anyone to appear.

I just fell into the creek climbing down a ladder to wade in the pool. My foot skidded on the slippery cement bottom and I splashed into shallow current. My notebook is soaked.

I've looped back to the bridge now, where the oak gall continues its circle-diving dance in the falls. My drenched dress clings to my calves. I realize I've become part of the action. I'm not just watching any more and that's where the poem hides, underwater where I slipped in, where my shadow joins the fishes, where *my* dress, blue and purple, is the reflected lily pad, where *I'm* the poem, outside of time, on a poem walk at One Mile.

2

Mr. Mabie

When I was fourteen I was in Jack Mabie's seventh/eighth-grade "pre-freshman" English class in the heart of the University of Chicago's neo-gothic campus. I'm sure there were windows, but I don't remember them. I don't even remember the room being attached to the rest of the Lab School. The class must have been upstairs in a distant wing of medieval Belfield Hall, far from the principal, the librarians and the metal rows of lockers—far from all the "shoulds" school meant to me.

Jack Mabie was short, buff and cocky. He had a blond, bristly crewcut and a smartass grin. He wore black-framed glasses sometimes and sunglasses sometimes. It was the sixties. Mr. Mabie claimed he wore "shades" because he couldn't stand the glare of our bright, shiny faces. He was hip.

I picture Mr. Mabie floating a few feet above me with a sarcastic smile, hovering like the Cheshire cat to my left. We sat in a rectangle of desks encircling the room. When Mr. Mabie sat down, he'd perch upright in a white shirt with sleeves rolled to his elbows and speak in a provocative yet relaxed city drawl. "susiegoldsmith," he called me, in a school packed with Sues.

Mr. Mabie brought out an irreverence never expressed in school, especially in me, small and mousy, with pointy blue glasses and frizzy hair, and redheaded Carola M., whom we called Squeegie. I remember Squeegie posing like Charlie Chaplin, handing Mr. Mabie an enormous box with a smaller box in a smaller box housing a tiny wad of paper with her thumbnail makeup report on *Agamemnon.*

Intentionally or not, Mr. Mabie created a field for poetry, a habitat for the nocturnal parts of our minds and psyches that tunnel around in the night searching out illuminated dreams. Mr. Mabie helped us burrow under and through the classroom that seemed both dark and light at the same time.

As I squint back at myself in that class, past the sky blue glasses, the shyness and flyaway hair, I catch my first glimpse of the person I am now. Somehow Mr. Mabie created a freedom that allowed me to emerge at fourteen, separating delicately, invisibly, from other people's ideas of the quiet, good girl I was *supposed* to be. A newly discovered part of me was set in motion, the person writing this page in this book; the part of me that writes poems.

That spring we began to read and write poetry in class. In addition, Mr. Mabie asked us to read the *Diary of Anne Frank* and begin daily journals in spiral notebooks. He promised not to read our journals aside from glancing at the pages upside down to check our progress, so I felt safe to record anything in mine. Writing in my journal, I felt an enormous kinship with Anne. My mother's maiden name is Frank. My grandfather Theodore Frank, like Anne, was from Frankfurt.

In my journal I began to feel free. I had round, wobbly script and sometimes I made stick and dot drawings in the margins. I survived school by developing a secret life in my journal. And I began to write poems in its pages. What made me feel like an outsider and an observer, different from others, could be poured into poems. Mr. Mabie even encouraged me to write poems rather than take his tests.

At the end of my first poem I enter a woods where I can see birds twittering happily and a little, lame squirrel collecting nuts. I closed,

> And I'm glad I can't understand their language
> for I sit down under a tree
> with an inchworm crawling up its side
> and at last I have peace, because I am unknowing.

I was looking for another language I didn't know yet. In Mr. Mabie's class I found the woods where I need to go to write poems. All these years later the journal is still my entrance. It seems dark the way a grove in the woods is dark. It's cool, safe, private, wide and free. It's green. In it there are iridescent beetles, wild roses, emus and other strange but real creatures, like me. All I needed to begin writing was freedom and white pages hiding in the dark of two covers.

PRACTICE

Buy yourself a notebook/journal that suits your personality and keep it with you, at least while you're reading this book. In a journal you can be self-centered and feel safe enough to write poems. It's never too late to start. Don't try to catch up by going back in your life. Start with now.

Some people like big, black sketch books with no lines. You might like pale graph paper lines, a marble-covered composition book like the one my friend Queenie has used for years, a spiral-bound watercolor book, a lined book with van Gogh or Matisse on the cover, or a small loose-leaf notebook like mine.

Sometimes I just carry a few folded pages in a dress purse, pony pack or shirt pocket. Writer Anne Lamott, who likes to spy and collect things the way I do, carries an index card or two because they fit in a back pocket of her jeans. "I learned to be like a ship's rat, veined ears trembling," Lamott writes in *Bird by Bird*, "and I learned to scribble it all down."

Be sure to use a pen or pencil you like. I like fountain pens, fine-point felt-tips with flowing black lines and Osmiroids, those fine-line graphic design fountain pens. I've even used a crow quill pen, a gull feather and a stick dipped in ink.

Begin now, even if you don't have a notebook yet. Scribble. Go for a walk and as you wander, take notes. Jot words anywhere. You can cut them out and tape them in your journal later.

3

collecting words and creating a wordpool

•

I have a strong gathering instinct. I collect boxes, hats, rusty flattened bottlecaps for collages and creek-worn sticks to color with my hoard of Berol prismacolor pencils. When I was a kid I'd lie in bed imagining I was a squirrel who lived in a hollow tree, foraging for acorns, twigs and whatever it takes to make squirrel furniture.

Most of us have collections. I ask people all the time in workshops, Do you collect anything? Stamps? Shells? '57 Chevys? Raccoons? Money? Leopards? Meteorites? Wisecracks? What a coincidence, I collect them, too. Hats, coins, cougars, old Studebakers. That is, I collect the *words*. Pith helmet, fragment, Frigidaire, quarrel, love seat, lily. I gather them into my journal.

The great thing about collecting words is they're free; you can borrow them, trade them in or toss them out. I'm trading in (and literally composting) some of my other collections—driftwood, acorns and bits of colored Easter egg shell—for words. Words are lightweight, unbreakable, portable, and they're everywhere. You can even make them up. *Frebrent, bezoncular, zurber.* Someone made up the word *padiddle.*

A word can trigger or inspire a poem, and words in a stack or thin list can make up poems.

Because I always carry my journal with me, I'm likely to jot down words on trains, in the car, at boring meetings (where I appear to be taking notes), on hikes and in bed.

I take words from everywhere. I might steal *steel,* spelled both ways. *Unscrupulous.* I'll toss in *iron, metal* and *magnolias.* Whatever flies into my mind. *Haystack, surge, sidewinder.* A sound, *splash.* A color, *magenta.* Here's a chair. *Velvet. Plush.*

Dylan Thomas loved the words he heard and saw around him in Wales. "When I experience anything," he once said, "I experience it as a thing and a word at the same time, both equally amazing." Writing one ballad, he said, was like carrying around an armload of words to a table upstairs and wondering if he'd get there in time.

Words stand for feelings, ideas, mountains, bees. Listen to the sound of words. I line up words I like to hear, *Nasturtiums buzz blue grass catnip catalpa catalog.*

I borrow words from poems, books and conversations. Politely. Take *polite.* If I'm in a classroom, I just start chalking them onto the board. I don't worry about spelling or meaning. *Curdle. Cantankerous. Linoleum. Limousine.* Listen. *Malevolent. Sukulilli,* the Maidu Indian word for silly. *Magnet cat oven taste tilt titter.*

I call gathering words this way creating a *wordpool.* This process helps free us to follow the words and write poems. In Paradise, California, my students and I looked up insects in a field guide with names like *firebrat, jumping bristletail* and *slantfaced grasshopper*. Then, moving around the room, I asked each person for one word, *any* word.

Everyone started tossing out words. *Tabulate. Magnify. Silence.* We could see the weight and value of each one. Someone said the word *no*. We put *yes* up there to balance it. Scott said *hate* and then *demolish*. We added *love* and *create* after talking about the importance of opposites. Then we looked for the opposite of *brick, idea, jealousy, tumbleweed* and *cloud*. We piled dozens of words on the board,

toe joust marvel
apparatus dome click
tubed tailstripes
flabbergast horse thought
cumulus cumulo nimbus
nom de plume zodiac zirconium flicker
slip spin serendipity
obsession pyromaniac two-tailed thrips
adobe hypothermia
frost dragon confetti tapioca
observe slither slink snuggle snooze

The rhythm, the music in the words, the circle of voices around the room, the associations, the well of minds casting out words like water in a fountain, words next to words in new ways and the look of them spreading across and down the page takes us to the state of mind poems come from.

I encourage people to toss foreign words into the wordpool. Just the sound can move us into another world very swiftly, like *avra*, breeze in Greek, or *petra*, rock. Add *petrified* and the Maidu word for water that sounds like a spring murmuring, *momoli*. Include place names like the ones I collected in Wales, *Abergavenny*, *Linthill* and *Skrinklehaven*.

Listed and tossed out this way, words begin to fall into poems by themselves. We put them together in unexpected ways, like *zodiac flicker, tree thought, tumbleweed sadness, magenta jealousy, cloud brick, summer ice, tapioca slithers.*

When I'm playing with words, I don't worry about sounding dumb or crazy. And I don't worry about whether or not I'm writing "a poem." *Word pool. World pool, wild pool, whipoorwill, swing.* Words taken out of the laborious structures (like this sentence) where we normally place them take on a spinning life of their own.

PRACTICE

Write words down. *Flap tip lob. Elope. Scrounge.*

Look around and steal some words. *Lamborghini. Jute. Wombat.*

Go ahead and make up a word. *Losoonie. Flapoon. Noplat.*

Be sloppy. Don't think. You can't make a mistake, there aren't any wrong words. *Phantom strut tumble porch. Dragoon.*

Don't worry too much about meaning for now. Words carry meaning along with them. Put words down and meaning will begin to rush in.

Give each word a color. *Vermilion regret.*

List the senses and give each sense a color. *Peach hearing.*

Toss in words from foreign languages. *Ciao.*

Go for sound: *hum, fizz, fiddle, fandango, zigzag, ziggurat, folderol, armadillo. Tintinabulation.*

Collect field guides. I often bring an insect, rock or butterfly book to workshops and we list words like *window winged moth, globular springtail* or *porphyry,* a purple rock named for the Latin and Greek word for "purple."

My friend Tom's Ford pickup repair manual is chock full of great words: *luminosity probe, diesel throttle control tool, acceleration pump link, swivel, internal vent valve, choke hinge pin . . .*

Look for a Magnetic Poetry Kit of words that stick to the refrigerator. My friend Arielle got a kit and told me, "Things just come out of you." She wrote about her family's twenty-one-year-old cat, Jumbo,

white puppy petal
you gorgeous milk fluff
sleep all day
lick tiny love from time
and dream

4

the answer squash

Sometimes I clip words, phrases and pictures from magazines to tape in my journal or arrange in collages. Once I clipped a rectangle of blue sky with a cloud trail and the words, *Do airplanes write your name in the sky?* For years I kept these clippings in a folder that came to mind as I drove home from my friend Jane's in Berkeley one fall, thinking about a seven-woman art show coming up. I'd agreed to a project blending sculpture and writing. I planned to label objects and I wanted the words to *look* good.

For years I'd scrawled words on index cards to hand out as writing tools in workshops. But now I wanted each word to be compact, forceful and beautiful. As I whizzed along the levee beside the Sacramento River past Glenn and Princeton, past groomed Mennonite farms, something made me think of tickets—the rolls you see at fairs and movie theaters. Maybe it was the giant Casino and Bingo Hall I passed outside of Colusa.

I could tape cut-out, printed words on tickets. Perfect, I thought. A ticket lets you *in* somewhere. On one side of some tickets it even says, "Admit one." Like a poem, a ticket is small, often colorful and valuable, allowing entrance to a special place.

When I got back to Chico, I found a big blue roll of tickets at Ellis Stationery, with the blank sides just waiting for a word or phrase. My two teenage kids helped me cut out words from a *New Yorker* story and tape them to tickets. *parachute. bamboo. black spaces.* The small, printed words gave the tickets a quiet, quirky authority, unlike words scribbled on cards. And stealing words from articles and poems felt like an adventure. We sat around the kitchen table excited about the words we clipped, including phrases like *searching hilarious, Lula let her cry, the first housekeeper* and *cold sheets.*

We went for nouns and verbs, gathering *daymoon, abandon, glow, jackhammer, extinguish, filter, China, contain, chamber.* Then the fun began, finding objects to label.

My son ransacked the garage and my daughter and I searched drawers and cabinets. We gathered an old globe, creek driftwood we'd colored with pencils, a pomegranate, a bristly magnolia seed pod, a scrub brush and a shoe, among other things. I added photographs and collages, one with oak galls. Another collage held firework remnants—burned and frayed rockets, chambers, tubes. Sometimes being a pack rat pays off.

We had a fine time labeling things. *Peach* went on the seed pod, *abandon boundary* on the globe, *sundial, north star, emperor, ruby* on the oak galls. My daughter picked *anger* (by chance) for the stump of a burned-out green candle. She reached into our pile of tickets and again by chance she picked *glow* for a white votive candle in a fragile dish. *Wolverine* was never placed.

Suddenly it seemed the objects could speak. They'd become poems themselves. Their labels changed the way we saw them. One of our favorite creations that afternoon was a squat, green squash with the label *answers* near its stem. *The answer squash,* we called it. My son's friend Gene was moved by a tattered green oak gall labeled *unreturnable love.* A colored piece of wood labeled *anchovy* invited close scrutiny, along with a pomegranate, *a mere lightbulb.* An enlarged photo of a key hole on a peeling door plate had the word *betray* pinned to it, and a worn scrub brush was labeled *diamonds.*

Is this play, poetry, art or silliness? Who cares? My kids were excited and involved, pinning words everywhere. I suspect I'll find labels on things around our house for months. I just found *hidden* in a bouquet of dried flowers and *frozen oceans* on a wooden dinosaur on the piano. These pieces are like small fragments of poems, word and object images speaking to us from around the house, as if they've popped out of a poetry book.

After my kids and I finished that afternoon, I gathered all the labeled things on a rickety, ancient card table and hauled it to the gallery as my contribution to the show. There was *Don't let nobody* speaking for a ragged, canvas gym shoe. *Grazing* defined an almond. *Let me be* spoke for a hammer.

At the show's opening on impulse I pinned *Rustproof* to a stiff fellow and soon people began choosing word tickets as name tags from a gold box purse. The room filled with people labeled *window, fortune, mingle* (who traded to get *mingle* twice and became *mingle mingle*), *ghost of the sun, searching hilarious* and *raccoon eyes.* One man pinned a row of words across his chest.

I noticed the new names seemed to change people. A shy, silent fellow got *underwater voices* and began to babble. Some people wanted to keep their labels. *Fortune* wore hers for weeks to bring her luck. As people moved into the mood of their labels, I began to see them as chatting fragments of poems I jotted into my journal.

"*Into the night,* with dark serious eyes," I recorded, "is whispering to *mars. Window* checks out the time, while *ultraviolet and ozone* leaves, looking suave in his long wool coat." Later I learned *ultraviolet*'s romance with *window* began that night. I've heard they're married now and have a baby.

PRACTICE

Tape words on tickets or on anything you want. My friend Andrea cuts up paint sample strips and tapes words above color names like *bluestone, jade* and *antique white*. She might end up with *pluck* over *forest green.*

Play with the word tickets. Pin or prop them around your house. I've got *smile* leaning up against my lamp. *Moonstone* peeks through the yellow plastic of my pen box.

Find unusual containers for your words. I had my word tickets in a hollow gourd until my dog, Emma, ate it, leaving chewed words in a swirl on the laundry room floor. Now I keep the tickets in a blue velvet pouch.

In your kitchen, writing room or car place bowls of words, boxes of them. Carry some in your purse or pocket, pull them out now and then and look at them. Words make great conversation.

Toss words, say them, sing them, chant, invoke, notice and let yourself get excited about them. My friends Rob and Chris lob words back and forth on car trips.

Collect nouns and verbs especially. We want the heart and guts: *blood, sweat* and *tears*. We want the action: *lure, slink, release, trickle, churn*.

Label things strangely. Put *lightning* on a shoe, *trigger* on a stone. Label a car, *spoon*. This turns everything upside down and loosens us up.

Pair verbs with nouns. You might wind up with a *tarantula spin* or *table exiting the long room*.

Collect words for things you love. Mix these with your verbs.

Gather words in an *ideals* envelope. Another envelope might contain *dreams* or all the names you'd like to give yourself: *star gazer, grass lover, clay spinner, poem catcher*. Fill a *wish* envelope.

If you're in a classroom, you might create a word ocean. Fill a fish tank with words.

Years ago poet Michael McClure suggested we each create our own "personal universe deck" of words in their simplest form on index cards. McClure suggested we include words of each sense, words of movement, body, time, place, an animal, a plant and at least one word that's an important abstraction, like *truth*.

See where your words take you.

5

most mad and moonly

Things I love have a way of turning up in my life in unexpected ways. In high school I idolized e. e. cummings because he was irreverent and made me feel free. He played with language and broke all the rules, nourishing my *Catcher in the Rye*, anti-establishment side.

I memorized most of "What of a much of a which of a wind" and several other cummings poems. My favorite for years was "Somewhere I have never traveled," with the unexpected line that moved me most, "and no one, not even the rain, has such small hands."

During my freshman year of college in New York City I met a Columbia student named Simon Roosevelt, who played Lysander in a production of *A Midsummer Night's Dream*. I painted viney leaves for the set as part of a stage crew that played loud rock music all hours of the night. I helped mend and fit costumes, happiest hanging out behind the scenes. Simon and I went to movies and studied together in the Columbia library. One evening I noticed a worn photo of e. e. cummings in Simon's wallet. "He was my grandfather," Simon told me. e. e. cummings—who died while I was in high school—was turning up again in my world. Life can be like a poem that way, with the unexpected appearing in the room, not just on the page.

cummings plays with words, spacing and capital letters, often putting all the punctuation somewhere unexpected. He experiments with opposites. His poems are both goofy and profound, soft and sharp at the same time, tender and fierce. "What of a much of a which of a wind" opens gently, but soon we're shocked as the wind "bloodies with dizzying leaves the sun / and yanks immortal stars awry."

cummings's words, often like the trail of an acrobat tumbling down the page, invite us to put our *own* words down. Filled with open, white space, his poems leave room for us to enter. We feel we can do this too. cummings's writing inspired a passion in me to create my *own* world, poke around and explore my boundaries, see how many shades of unnamed color and sound I might find there.

I write this in the car as we zoom home from Berkeley approaching—believe it or not—the "Cummings Skyway." Here's Crockett, where the world opens up like a cummings poem into sky, water, sun, ships, and we soar over the Carquinez Strait high in ocean air on a towering erector-set bridge. Back home, my teenage daughter saunters into my room with her hair in a high bun, shoulders low, lips pouting, hips swaying. She's a feminist high-fashion model named Tangerine Valentino. Now she swivels out, ignoring my applause, creating a character sketch for her drama class.

cummings reminds me to allow poems to swagger, soar or tiptoe in unexpectedly. I need to be open and ready for them. Poems aren't written from ideas, like essays, and they're not overly controlled. In a poem's "most mad and moonly" spell, out of time, I can break rules and expectations about who I am as well as about writing.

My journal has a memorial page both for e. e. cummings and for his grandson Simon, killed on his red motorcycle the year after we met. At Simon's memorial service someone read a cummings poem that helped us with our shock and sadness,

love is more thicker than forget
more thinner than recall
more seldom than a wave is wet
more frequent than to fail

it is most mad and moonly
and less it shall unbe
than all the sea which only
is deeper than the sea

love is less always than to win
less never than alive
less bigger than the least begin
less littler than forgive

it is most sane and sunly
and more it cannot die
than all the sky which only
is higher than the sky.

The unexpected brings us light and darkness, joy and sorrow, life and death. And it brings discovery. Some of our most important discoveries are made when we're not looking.

PRACTICE

Read some poems by e. e. cummings.

Let a poem write itself as if you were taking dictation from your pen.

Break words up.

Frag
men
t

Let yourself be like a kid. Write your name some way you've never written it before. *Draw* your name. Use colored pens or pencils.

Go somewhere outside and turn over a stone.

List in detail what's under the stone that you didn't expect.

Notice three new things in someone's face. Write down what you've seen.

Notice anything that spirals, from the corkscrew to the pasta to the weather patterns on the news.

Write a series of images without stopping. Make some of them absurd. *The snow is black today. It's been raining paint. My dog is singing* La Bohème.

Give colors to ideas and abstractions. *Blue love. Chartreuse agreements. Silver deliberation. Magenta pride.*

Be open to unexpected words and adventures. Spend time being in a state of quiet expectation and see what (or who) comes your way.

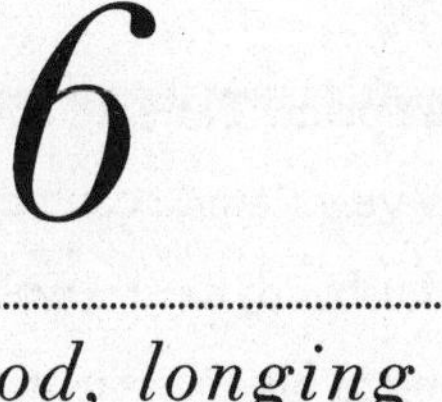

gas, food, longing

I could glimpse the Hudson River bordering New Jersey when I lived in the Barnard College dorm. This glimpse filled me with longing for I wasn't sure what—maybe a houseboat on the river, a village life I loved or the person I knew I could be.

One weekend I went to a van Gogh exhibit at the Guggenheim Museum. As I rounded a curve in the gallery I saw a painting called *The Sower*. A faceless man, solid as the tree leaning toward him, scatters seeds near a river lit by a huge sun, palpable as a grapefruit in a green sky.

Staring at the painting, I almost stopped breathing. The simple figure in sunset seeding the earth expressed all my feelings of longing, hope and promise. I felt van Gogh had painted the inside of *me*. *I* was the peasant expectantly seeding the field. *I* was the glimpse of river like a blue path. *I* was the low sun about to sink from sight. *I* was the seed in a dark hand waiting to be tossed home.

Though it cost more than I could afford, I bought a print of *The Sower* at the show and hung it on a straw mat in my pale green dorm room. The painting made me feel less alone, though I never lost that longing. Even now on the freeway sometimes I'll read the signs as, "Gas, Food, *Longing.*"

I still have that print. Tattered and ripped, it's tacked to a wall in the garage, so many years later. I can't throw it out. When I left Barnard and met my future husband, Kent, I was delighted to see a paler version of my *Sower* hanging in his apartment.

For years I've collected paintings on postcards my friend Deborah sends me. I have a large shoebox full. There's Ivan Albright's door, crumbling and bedecked with fading roses like a poem that makes me feel loss and regret.

Albright gave his painting a name that's a poem fragment in itself, *That Which I Should Have Done I Did Not Do.* There's a Magritte room that makes me feel expansive with its clouds for walls, giant comb and shaving brush. Once a student saw this painting and, using the word tickets, wrote, "Suddenly my walls disappear."

In workshops I give each student a postcard to transform into a painting with words. Creating an image with words can express a feeling with color flooding in, as van Gogh's painting does for me.

Image is the root word of imagination. It's from the Latin *imago,* "picture," how you see things. Images carry feelings. Saying, "I'm angry," or "I'm sad," has little impact. Creating images, I can make you feel how I feel.

When I read the words of a young student named Cari—"I'm a rose in the shape of a heart / with nineteen days of nothing / but the pouncing of shoes on my dead petals"—I experience desperation through her image. Cari doesn't even have to name the feeling. It's often details that carry feeling—nineteen days, a pale green sky, a pouch of seeds held against a sower's heart.

Writing poems using images can create an experience allowing others to feel what we feel. Perhaps more important, poems can put us in touch with our own often buried or unexpected feelings.

Shoua discovered her frustration by using the image of a man shooting pool,

> I hear bang, click, shoosh
> feeling like the white ball
> that does all the work.

Tori used images from a landscape to indicate hopelessness.

> the clouds collapsed,
> they're touching the ground
> trying to come alive,
> but they can't.

Sometimes word tickets magically fit with the images in the paintings. One of Tori's words was *jingle*. It helped her convey her developing feeling of hope,

> the glowing water shows shadows
> till we all hear
> the *jingle* of dawn.

Images we create in our poems can not only help us discover our feelings, but can help us begin to transform them.

PRACTICE

Make a wordpool of feeling words, going for opposites: *psychotic stable laughable sober drab vibrant bored blissful frantic calm fragile invincible.*

Find a postcard of a painting, a reproduction in a magazine or book, or a poster on a wall. Any painting will do.

Choose a feeling. Look closely at your painting and find a detail that seems to express your feeling, perhaps one color or the gesture of someone's arm. Perhaps a jug in the corner. Let your words paint the feeling. *I feel as still as a white water jug.*

Say your painting is a landscape. You feel *powerless.* What does that grey cloud look like that expresses your feeling? You might write that the cloud is dissolving, losing its shape. Or you feel *powerful.* Now the cloud is gathering electricity to snap out as lightning.

You might feel *unimportant,* like that tiny leaf on top of the tree, lost in all the others. You might feel you're *fading* like the last bit of pink light on top of the mountain.

Choose a variety of paintings so you can begin to express the full range of your feelings in one or several poems.

7

being here

Once I heard poet Gary Snyder say, "Poetry has an interesting function. It helps people *be* where they are." It's hard to write a poem about a place, an experience or even a state of mind without fully *being* there. When I'm fully present describing a place in a poem it helps bring my reader there too.

I need to breathe in the air, hear the sounds, feel the ground under my feet and join a place to fully describe it. If it's winter, my footprints need to sink in snow or mud beside weblike bird tracks. I need to get wet or muddy, smell, taste and look at things closely. It's important for me to use all my senses in poems: sight, touch, smell, taste, hearing and the sixth sense, intuition or "dreamsense," as my friend Mark Rodriguez calls it.

Yesterday morning, on a walk, my writing partner Elizabeth and I got so caught up talking about our kids we barely noticed we were walking along the creek. To write poems I need to be alone. When I avoid being alone I avoid poetry and the messages it brings me.

Alone I open my senses, listen to my surroundings, take in the smells, the light and the way a sycamore curves over the creek like a pale rainbow. "Everything's got to do with listening," the poet W. S. Merwin said of a poem he wrote about the wind. Many of my poems come from what I notice when I'm alone.

Writer Louis Owens says that to most Native Americans, paying this kind of attention is a responsibility. "Our job is to be an awake people . . . utterly conscious, to attend to our world."

This noon I'm on the upper park rim trail on a pockmarked rock. It rained yesterday and there's a veil of mud over the lava cap on the ridge. My dog, Emma, explores as I peer over star thistle at retreating clouds. Thin winter grass is poking up and it's mid-November. Soon I'll find miner's lettuce to feed my kids along with the curly dock I gather for my daughter and me. Everyone else thinks it's too sour.

To experience a place I need to walk in it as often as I can. Abenaki native poet Joseph Bruchac says, "We need to walk to know sacred places, those around us and those within. We need to walk to remember the songs."

Now I've climbed up the hill about fifty feet and I'm sitting against an oak. I'm holding two large acorn caps like small pipe bowls. Here's one of the acorns, long, greenish brown. I rub off the tiny point and polish the acorn with my fingers. Later at home, two acorns will wobble around on the kitchen table shining like bullets.

Bird song. Sweet air. I feel the crumbly oak bark against my back. A darting bird's just above me and I hear thrumming wings. The oak helps me trust and wait and breathe and bend. I feel my body and mind taking in the tree. Soon I'll see what words come.

For now, I'll just *be here*, alone, watching and listening.

PRACTICE

All my poems are suggested by real life and therein have a firm foundation. . . . No one can imitate when you write of the particular, because no others have experienced exactly the same thing.

—Goethe

Walk somewhere alone. Listen. Write about what's around you, using all of your senses.

It's important to narrow everything down, make it as specific as you can, down to the tip of a blade of grass, or you'll leave the reader out. For emotion to arise, writing has to be very specific—describing a particular moment or experience in a particular place.

A useful daily practice is to sit (or walk) with a notebook and focus on what's happening right now, in minute detail. "Inside a moment," Emily Dickinson wrote, "centuries of June."

Wherever you are, if it's warm enough, take off your shoes. Breathe deeply. What can you smell?

Look to your right. What's there? Feel your body and mind taking it in.

Look straight down. Notice a color, texture, shape.

Look straight up. Do you see acoustical tiles or blue sky or antique white plaster? Is there a spider up there in a corner webbing herself over? Leave her there, but describe her exactly on paper.

William Blake thought that art and science exist in the organization of "Minute Particulars." Blake saw "a World in a Grain of Sand."

Listen. Do you hear a coffeemaker? Freeway sounds? Tree frogs?

Place your right hand down. What do you feel? A nubby cushion, a chair? Your knee in frayed leggings?

Look closely at something you see all the time. Write as if you've never seen this before.

Keep writing. If you focus on your surroundings, the words may just help you be there. But if they want to take you somewhere else, follow them.

8

it looks like

When my son, Daniel, was small he would often compare the way one thing looked to another. Passing a peach cannery I said, "See the smoke coming out of that chimney?" Daniel responded, "Just yike a cigarette." He was always saying, *"It yooks yike, it yooks yike."* When his sister, Elisabeth, was born, Dan saw her swaddled with only her head visible and remarked, "She yooks yike a hot dog."

When we transplanted a small tree from a pot to a hole in the ground, Daniel said, "The world will be its new pants." As we drove toward the coast one day and saw cows on the hillside, Elisabeth said, "They yook yike popcorn."

I think we naturally see things metaphorically. We're always comparing the way one thing looks to another. Comparison is built into our language.

I've noticed that on a highway a hairpin turn, from above, *looks like* a hairpin. Cattails in a swampy area along Lonestar Road *look like* cat's tails. In my garden foxglove looks like a wee "folk's glove," with a pouch for a tiny hand. Georgia O'Keeffe said she painted individual flowers and made them huge so we'd be forced to look closely and notice what flowers really look like. Whether she intended this or not, O'Keeffe's paintings lend themselves to metaphor. Inside her white flower I see

> a gown with long white sleeves,
> a curled satin slipper with grey on the toe,
> a Chinese lantern on low,
> a bowl of silver bells, ringing.

Wilfred Funk writes in *Word Origins and Their Romantic Stories* that originally all words were poems, since our language is based, like poems, in metaphor. The names of flowers makes this easier to see. This flower looks like a shooting star. Maybe the next time I see one I'll make the shift from simile to full metaphor and think, This flower *is* a shooting star, or a bird's-eye, a paintbrush, butter and eggs.

In some words we can still see the poem/metaphor, especially flowers and trees like ladyslipper, redbud, spinster blue-eyed Mary. My married name, Wooldridge, must have come from the image of lambs on a ridge.

Metaphor is a bridge bringing things together. The world is a stage. Life is a dream. The navel is a belly button. When she lived in Athens years ago, a friend Sally tells me, some of the delivery bikes had the word METAPHOR printed on their sides—probably a company name. In Greek *metaphor* literally means to bear or carry over.

Sometimes part of writing a poem is as simple as looking carefully and bringing things together through simile and metaphor. This bit of moon looks like a canoe. The moon *is* a cradle, a wolf's tooth, a fingernail, snow on a curved leaf or milk in the bottom of a tipped glass.

PRACTICE

Take an object and think about what it *looks like*. Describe exactly what you see.

Look around you. Does your lampshade look like a ballerina's illuminated pink pleated skirt? Not exactly, but it's a start. Let yourself go for the farfetched and the ridiculous when you make comparisons.

If you can find a flower, look inside. What does it look like?

Find a painting, abstract or realistic. Choose a detail and stare at it. Focusing on that detail, write,

I see
it looks like

it looks like

I see

It looks like (repeat)

For more practice, list what you see around you and write down what it looks like.

The pine tree looks like a torpedo

That folded piece of paper looks like a flattened sail

The curled telephone cord looks like an earthworm

That man's curly hair looks like . . .

The moth's wing . . .

Keep going.

9

naming wild hippo

My dog, Emma, and I have been galumphing in the park. On the rim trail Monday I saw the first spring shooting star and yellow carpet. Most of my walking is done in Bidwell Park, which stretches into the Sierra Nevada foothills alongside Chico Creek, becoming "Upper Park." Errol Flynn's *Robin Hood* was filmed in the oaks and the wild grapevines here. When my children were little

I brought wildflower books on family hikes in the park until I realized my obsession with the name of each flower was ruining our walks.

For better or worse, by then we could recognize *fiddle neck, stork bill, butter and eggs* (also called *johnny tuck*), *gold field, yellow carpet, brodiea, seepspring monkey flower, Indian paintbrush, tidy tips, popcorn flower, shooting star, birdseye (gilia)* and *owls clover,* among others.

The names helped us see the flowers, their sharp bird's eyes in gilia's blue lids, their tidy tips and their monkey cheeks.

My friend Chris says a woodland plant identification course changed her life. It reminded her of getting glasses in the sixth grade and suddenly seeing each rock that made up the gravel. Before the plant class, Chris says, "The woods were all just kinda green." After the class Chris saw *bunchberry, bedstraw, miner's lettuce, twinflower, twisted stalk* and *goat'sbeard.*

John Lust's *Herb Book* is full of wonderful names like the common ones for flowering spurge: *bowman's root, emetic root, milk ipecac, milk purslain, milkweed* and, do you believe it? *wild hippo.* The name makes me see a bulbous, gray-green plant wallowing in water.

Once a long time ago someone looked closely and named these plants as he or she saw or experienced them, pinning and narrowing them down with words: *checkerberry, deerberry, hive vine, one-berry, star grass, colic root* and *star root.*

Not only can we see a thing more clearly when it has a name, we have access to it, a way of calling it forth and connecting with it. It becomes more particular in relation to us and in a way it becomes ours.

Many Native Americans understand this and won't give their

name to a stranger. The last California Yahi Indian, Ishi, didn't reveal his personal name when he came to live in Berkeley in 1911. The name he used, Ishi, simply means *man* in his native language.

A name can also alter, limit or expand the way we see what's named. Last week I watched a juggler using rods to toss other rods like wands over his head at One Mile. I asked if there was a name for the sticks clicking in the air. In America, he said, they're called "Twiddle Sticks." That's innocent enough. But in China, he explained, where the sticks come from, they're called either *devil sticks* or *flower sticks.*

When the juggler said *devil sticks* my perception shifted and for a moment the sticks looked sharp and their clatter sounded sinister. When he called them *flower sticks,* the rods suddenly looped into a daisy in the air.

Names are powerful. They influence our perception. The Chinese master Confucius believed all wisdom came from learning to call things by the right name.

PRACTICE

Take a walk somewhere outside.

Pretend you're the first person who has ever seen the plants and trees on this walk. It's your job to name them.

Notice each type of tree. What does it look like? Is there something distinctive about the leaves or the shape of the trunk? Name each tree.

Name the plants you see. Name the bugs.

Name spots you like to go on your walks, gardens, beaches, sections of town that are special to you.

Name your car and your bicycle.

Rename your street.

Walk at night, especially when the moon is almost full. Go uphill.

Rename the stars, the moon.

Rename the sky.

IO

our real names

Susan's a fine name. But everywhere I go I meet at least two Susans about my age. Last week at my friend Jane's party there were four of us in practical shoes, holding forth with firm opinions. I'd prefer to be named Manuela or Tess. For years I was Sue and I was only able to slip into Susan when we moved to Chico. My mother, who is resigned to her name Ethel, put up with *Tootsie* for years until college and then dutifully went back to Ethel. Her brother was stuck with *Elmore*—created from the names Elijah, Moses and Theodore—until his early death. Sometimes I think his name killed him. And I can't even *imagine* how my mother's grandfather in Germany felt about being named Falk Falk. Didn't his parents understand that one Falk was enough?

When he was a boy in Oak Park, Illinois, my father, Julian, told new friends his name was Roy (for his middle name, Royce). When the kids came by to ask Roy to play fireman, his mother (Celia) put an end to Julian's quiet rebellion by saying no one named Roy lived with *her*.

Our culture doesn't make changing names easy. My friend Elizabeth had a hard time reclaiming her full name after years of Betty. I think Jay, a writer, has given up on the name Lucky, and my African dance teacher Jeanne has let go of Jamaica, at least for now. A friend who was Els has managed to become Karisa, but it took her six years.

Among some tribal people names change when character-evolving events take place. Members of an aborigine tribe take on a new name when they feel ready for one. They keep their birth name until five or six and then choose a name based on a talent or interest. They'll hold a party to declare their new name, which may be something like "Interested in Wood." A few years later they may hold another party and become "Boomerang Maker" and, eventually, "Number One Whizbang Boomerang Maker." They'll declare they've undergone a transformation and honor this with a name to help everyone see them in a new way.

"A name should be taken as an act of liberation, of celebration, of intention," writes Erica Jong in *Fear of Fifty*. "A name should be a magical invocation to the muse. A name should be a self-blessing."

Poetry can be about discovering and naming ourselves. And creating a name can be like writing a poem. In a small group at the Juvenile Hall one day we decided to rename ourselves. We talked about what our *real* name might be or how we might name ourselves in different situations. What is the name that truly expresses who and where you are right now?

Young people in the Juvenile Hall are used to the idea of an alias. They call themselves nicknames like Pony Boy, Jude, Angel, Roly Poly, La Vicious, Homesick, Sober, Storm, Desperado, Joe Mama and Dalimar.

Chao, an Asian gang leader, was pleased to hear that an "s" at the end of his name creates Chaos—a word that seemed to him *close* to his real name. At first he wasn't sure what chaos meant and loved hearing Milton's definition, "Chaos, that vast, immeasurable abyss, outrageous as the sea—dark, wasteful, wild." Kenny, a Chicano gang leader, stole "abyss" from Milton to use in a poem about *his* real name.

Everyone liked the idea of using word tickets and chose a name or two from the pool. Kenny drew ***dogstar***. Perfect. He's a dog, he's a star. Ronnie picked ***helium dream***. Then we came up with opening lines, including

> My real name is
> yesterday my name was
> today my name is
> tomorrow my name will be
> secretly I know my name is
> My name once was

Using the word tickets and these opening lines, the students wrote poems about their real names. Ronnie especially felt he *needed* a new name. Pale, tall, blue-eyed, blond, he was ashamed of the words ***white*** *power* his uncle had tattooed on his shoulder when he was eight. Ronnie was about to be released into the difficult world outside the hall, where he's seen as an illiterate delinquent with a child, a wife and a history. He dictated this to me nervously, offhand:

> Let's talk about death.
> Yesterday my name was James.
> Today it's tossing helium dream.
> Tomorrow my name will be
> Gerald Flying off the Cliff,
> Dave Mustang.
> Inside my name is
> dying heart,
> sorrow
> guilt
> and a lotta hope.

PRACTICE

Use word tickets to help get you started creating new names for yourself. Try some of these starters:

> My real name is
> yesterday my name was
> tomorrow my name will be
> in my dream my name was
> my husband, mother, son, boss (etc.), thinks my name is

Always listen for the opposite. If you're getting serious, let yourself become silly. If you're getting silly, become serious. Pile on name after name to see what emerges. Break rules. Surprise yourself. Your new name might be *breaker of green rules, surrounded by wasps.*

My colleague Gail named the part of her that writes *Minerva.* The old folks in her neighborhood saw her wisdom and told her parents, "You got a little Minerva on your hands." The name stuck.

In a backyard writing workshop Jeri, a teacher, wrote,

> Yesterday my name was seaweed.
> Tomorrow my name will be
> hot-hipped black woman.
> I will plant each bare foot firmly
> and pollinate the radiant air
> with my humming.

You may want more than one name for your different sides and moods and names to change with the seasons. Sometimes your name may be *mint taking over,* or *mantis on the rose bush.* Sometimes *Manuela.* Sometimes *Mary.*

APOLOGY

A word sticks in the wind's throat;
A wind-launch drifts in the wells of rye;
Sometimes, in broad silence,
The hanging apples distil their darkness.

You, in a green dress, calling, and with brown hair,
Who come by the field-path now, whose name I say
Softly, forgive me love if also I call you
Wind's word, apple-heart, haven of grasses.

—*Richard Wilbur*

II

opening shots

•

There's a "very tiny crack in which another world begins and ends."
—Slavko Mihalic

I'm by the trunk of a small oak, looking up into the branches, and I realize I've had the same thought over and over for years: This would make a great *opening shot* for a movie. I want to bring people into this rooted haven nothing can blow away, an enclosed world of limbs and leaves still enough for moss and lichen.

I wish I could remember all the opening shots I've noticed. I just now saw one of my old opening shots on TV—a pilot's view of flying through billowing clouds. A lot of my opening shots have water in them. In a special on Monty Python last night there was my shot of light on lake water rippling with the credits flashing by. Another shot is water splashing from the faucet of an old sink. Hundreds of shots I've noticed have slipped away, openers that can take me somewhere, like portals to another dimension.

This morning downtown I saw pigeons flying in an opening shot like the cells of a single organism moving under a microscope. *Pigeons*. Silver, black, silver. *Flash. Swoop*. Roll the cameras.

In Chicago's O'Hare Airport I recently experienced an opening shot that takes place in a passageway—perfect, because an opening shot moves us between two worlds. In this complicated shot of a moving walkway, wiry looping lines in changing neon colors are reflected on a ceiling mirror, rubber armrails and stone floors. The walls are glowing colored light in frosted glass.

Like a poem, this walkway is clearly a corridor to another world. When you look up, you see yourself upside down, feet striding on the ceiling among strangers rushing luggage from one realm to another.

For me it's not always enough to simply experience what I see in the moment, like the last light on catalpa blossoms high on our neighbor's tree. It's not always enough for me to notice things, enjoy them and take them in, like O'Hare's moving walkway. I want to bring someone else there also to experience a neon hall of mirrors or a luminous fog or rain.

In a poem I can catch the opening shot with words and it becomes an invitation, a passageway deeper into the experience, just as the opening shot in a film invites us into the larger world of a movie. Like movies, poems create an experience rather than report one. As Archibald MacLeish wrote in his "Ars Poetica," "a poem should not mean, but *be*."

In poems we're moved to catch the moment or place inside or outside ourselves where something is different and we know we're about to be led somewhere new. An opening may be all we need to take us. We don't know where we'll be and that's the joy of it. And often we want to bring someone along.

12

on a night picnic

Our family friend Chris loves to create small occasions. Last year at her cabin on Puget Sound in Washington, Chris suggested my daughter, Elisabeth, and I go on a night picnic with her in the red canoe beside the deck. The tide goes in and out below this deck and sometimes we see seals where a front lawn would normally be. When the tide's out during the day we explore the stretch of shore finding clay babies, crabs, oysters and brittle, white sand dollars that are black and bendable when they're alive.

This August night with the tide in we prepared three cups of Long Life tea, lined the canoe with blankets and towels and took off, each holding a citronella candle on a wooden stick. We were planning to watch the meteor showers forecast on the news. After paddling out and drinking tea, we blew out the candles to watch and drift on the sound. We began to sing "Catch a Falling Star." On the deck the night before, the song often seemed to bring a flash in the sky. It was more of a meteor *drip* than a shower.

Out in the canoe we saw very few shooting stars. But Elisabeth noticed that whenever we moved a paddle or hand in the water it lit up as if Tinker Bell had sprinkled magic light into the sound. The starry show turned out to be beneath, not above us—from phosphorescent plankton. The ocean was alive and filled with light.

Sometimes we think poems need to be about important, dramatic moments. The events of our lives seem mundane. Often the small occasions in the front or back yard are the most magical. We just need to notice and then create a way to experience and enjoy this ordinary magic.

PRACTICE

Do what our friend Chris does and create a small occasion.

Look for a moment that can be made into an event.

Celebrate the full moon with a hike somewhere in the open at night. Arrange a gathering at sunset and sing lullabies or make toasts as the sun disappears.

Include candles, a fire or sparklers and something to drink. Think of props to make each experience unforgettable—fireworks, boots or floating flowers and unusual foods.

Look up the birthday of a favorite writer and gather friends to read poems or stories.

Make someone's birthday cake into a poem. For her father Stanton's birthday tomorrow, my friend Arielle and her mother Joann are decorating a cake encased in marzipan with gold-leaf letters. "You can eat gold," Arielle insists. Using gathered words they wrote a poem for the cake's top.

A yellow gift
imagines its joy
rounding a bubble
tinting a peach
thinking sky.
It lands
hot on 53 years
and celebrates.

We can make a small occasion large by the focus of our attention, by the reverence and excitement we bring to it.

Set your occasion in motion and see what comes of it.

Then write.

2

Listening to ourselves

13

the poemfish

Recently another writer and I read some poems to an audience at Chico State University. It had been a stormy day. The weather went from pouring to sunny to windy to hailing to still. A tornado in nearby Oroville leveled a few houses.

The room was crowded, with a few people even peering through the door in back. I read second and turned the lights low. I'd brought three candles and a floor lamp from home. Sparks from a faulty wick flew onto the rug and my friend Lew scampered around like a bearded imp, putting them out. I talked about my poems being messages from me to myself. I read poems I've written in my sleep, in the car and one or two written when I was both stationary and awake. My friend Diane laughed loud at just the right times. My husband Kent was there and our friends Buck and Ellen ambled in. I *stayed* with *myself.* I felt free to risk being the oddball I often think I am. I even dared play the harmonica, briefly.

I felt like a star. I read an encore, fittingly a poem called "The Fool." It seemed as if my life was changing on the spot. A train to take me to the Copacabana was on its way to the door of BMU 222. But soon the room emptied. Someone spilled water from Wendy's vase of flowering quince on the rug and it looked like a dog had peed in front of the podium, shedding pink petals at the same time.

There sat my unruly basket with a Paul Newman salsa jar half full of wine for nerves, candles, my harmonica and long branches of quince. There was my old floor lamp softening the light. Joanne and Andrea helped me lug these things to the parking lot just in time to avoid a ticket. I gave the traffic cop a branch of quince. A few of us went to Cafe Phoenix, where Frank Ficarra was starring with his jazz band. My moment was over.

At home, the kitchen was a mess. There were heaps of clothes in my bedroom from my scramble with Tanha for a sexy and sophisticated but casual outfit. My daughter was at a friend's. She had no idea her mother was a brilliant performer. Kent was ensconced in his green velvet chair in a corner of the den, reading Updike. My son was on the town after a drama class performance of his own.

Oh well. I'm still the same person, perched in the same life. I guess I can write and read until I'm blue in the face to standing-room-only crowds that are cheering and throwing flowers and my *life* won't change unless I do the changing. The poems really are messages to me whispering, Be calm, go deep, go slow. There's a long poem brewing in me, *The Poemfish*, still rough,

> . . . When the poemfish moves
> the sea lights up
> with stars that dip and swim . . .
> The poemfish lives
> in the night ocean.
> If you sleep mouth open
> the poemfish might swim in.
> You'll dream salty words
> that swim away sideways, slow. . . .

And now I remember. Worrying about what people think of me and my poems always gets me in trouble. I get lost "out there." It's the process of *writing poems* that helps me bring my heart back home. It puts me in touch with the ocean inside I can never lose, where poems come from and where I connect with *me*.

14

full moon me

As I write I create myself again and again.
—Joy Harjo

The opening entry in my diary at fifteen reads, "Dedicated to me. To the me of the future." And my most recent journal entry is about me on a walk in the park with my dog, Emma: "Dozens of swallows were lined up this morning like plump clothespins on the powerlines. They flew to greet Emma and me as we climbed up the road from the creek. The swallows may have had other business, but this felt like a benediction—white breasted birds swooped close and circled as if garlanding us with invisible ribbons."

Not only am I writing about myself here, but I see the whole world as centered around me. Writing about ourselves doesn't mean we're self-involved. We have to start with ourselves before we can reach beyond ourselves. And whatever our intention, the way we see and write about the world always reveals who we are.

I love to write about myself and I think most people do. It's one of the major impulses in poetry throughout history—from Sappho and

Ovid to St. Augustine and the modern poets. And there's a part of every poet that's crazy about the sound of his or her own words. My friend Jack Grapes playfully parodies this tendency:

> I like my own poems
> best.
> I quote from them
> from time to time
> saying "A poet once said,"
> and then follow up
> with a line or two from one of my own poems
> appropriate to the event.
> How those lines sing! . . .

Jack celebrates the love we have for our own words, a reflection of our love for ourselves and excitement about what our poems can bring. Poems aren't simply bits of art to be whittled to perfection and admired or revered. They're ground troopers with laser beams illuminating caverns within. They can bring messages from and about our deepest selves, broadening our respect and reverence for who we are.

We can make discoveries when we put our feelings about ourselves in words. David in the Juvenile Hall school found (and revealed) the rose hiding inside the gangster,

> I'm a brown gangster
> colliding with death
> a rose slamming love
> with hate.

"Did I write that?" another young man asked in the Juvenile Hall school when visiting singer Stevie Cook wailed out the words he'd composed,

I'm a frozen rain
a river without motion
a runner stopped,
a car dead. . . .

The young man was touched and perhaps moved to compassion for himself by the power of his own words. He was also able to witness how much his words moved others.

In poems we can not only discover more about who we are and how we feel, we can learn to like ourselves. Fourth-grader Daniel was able to experience a freeing exuberance about himself in a poem with phrases like *mad star bones, camouflage grandma* and *September Peach.* He closed his poem with the words,

I'm a weird mad man,
full moon me.

PRACTICE

I often use this practice in my first workshop session, after we've collected a lot of words. Jot down in a list the first thing you see when you ask yourself,

If I were a color, what color would I be? (From red to the inside-of-a-watermelon-seed color.)

What shape would I be? (Whatever you see—an airplane wing shape, a boot shape, a parallelogram, a cone, a diamond.)

If I were a movement, what movement would I be? (glide, hop, wiggle, spin)

What sound?

What animal?

What song?

What number? (infinity, googolplex, eight, sixteen)

What car? (Details: year, color, condition)

What piece of furniture?

What food?

What musical instrument?

What place?

What element in nature? (dust, galaxy, waterfall)

What kind of a tree?

What's something I'm afraid of?

What's the word hiding behind my eyes?

Put down the words *I am . . .*

Write about yourself using answers to the questions above as well as action words you've collected—*spin clarify fiddle fling dribble lunge slug slam spiral rehearse splurge balance value love leap stop reply . . .*

A young man named Kenya wrote, *I'm a turquoise circle, rolling into nowhere, / . . . I'm the number 50, so far from the end and far from the beginning. . . . I'm what you call life, hard to hold.*

Just pile on words. *Don't think.* See images. Daydream with words. Wander. Go crazy defining yourself, like seventh-grader

Paul, who filled a page with lines like, *"I'm a space closet opposite/bummed cold fire. . . ."* Use the wordpools in this book and all the words you've collected so far. There are no rules and there's no audience. Be silly, serious, wry or overdramatic.

If you get tired of *I am,* start lines with

I will be
I want to be
I used to be
I let go of
I've forgotten
I remember

—as long as you're writing about yourself.

In a college class of teachers-in-training last week, Del said he hated doing this, it seemed forced and contrived. But then he couldn't stop writing. He went home and returned with several typed pages filled with lines like,

I'm September solid.
We're the flat-bottomed tree,
alchemists turning limestone into solar wind . . .

This practice works for all ages. Jessica, a fourth-grader, wrote,

I'm a poem that flies through the sky
I'm love and truth,
happy and sad
three dreams,
porcelain and fragile
in the night.

I never tire of these *I am* poems in workshops. Most of us are amazed by ourselves and each other—our depth, breadth, silliness, sadness and all we have in common. So much comes tumbling out, as if we've been given a brush to paint a larger picture of ourselves.

In your notebook keep gathering words to write an ongoing, lifelong, rolling, ever-changing *I am* poem.

15

Walt Whitman

The summer I was sixteen I hid out in a hollow in the pine trees near Little Sissabagama, a lake in northern Wisconsin where my family vacationed every summer. I was a certified would-be early bohemian, barefoot in cut-off jeans and a blue denim workshirt, dubbing myself "blue goldsmith." I wanted to read, write and figure out who I was.

My hip romantic interest Richard B. gave me the first slim edition of Allen Ginsberg's *Howl,* and Walt Whitman's words on Ginsberg's title page described how I felt about writing and life. "Unscrew the locks from the doors. Unscrew the doors themselves from their jambs!"

That summer I decided to live a life of letters. I began writing in the first of the loose-leaf notebooks I call "my little black books."

They're four-by-six with six rings holding paper with skinny blue lines I still find inviting. I began carrying a little black book with me everywhere, as I've done ever since. No one knows what I'm writing in such ordinary books. They allow me to feel secret and wild, the way I need to feel to write poems.

I read *The Confessions of Jean-Jacques Rousseau,* awed by Rousseau's pledge to write truthfully about his experience. I still have the pale blue and pea green paperback. And I still have the same old copy of *The Whitman Reader* with a pensive, soulful Walt on the sepia cover.

I wrote rambling odes of praise to Whitman in my journal and with my Brownie camera I photographed his book propped against tall grasses in my hollow. Later I taped these photos into my black book.

I loved everything Whitman said to me in my secret hollow by the lake. I knew I wanted a life free and full of poetry and adventure like his,

> Done with indoor complaints, libraries, querulous
> criticisms,
> Strong and content I travel the open road.

I wanted to live in a world of freedom I could only find in poems. Along with Whitman, who saw poetry everywhere, and e. e. cummings, I was excited about Dylan Thomas, who, if not free, at least "sang in his chains like the sea." I was becoming wordmad, poemcrazy. Reading these poets changed me, as did Amy Lowell with her moving poem "Patterns," and Emily Dickinson, who defined her own life, love and freedom with words: "My business is circumference."

I wanted to escape the ordinary life I thought my parents were living so I could hang out with poets, writers and artists at the inner frontier. I wanted to leap into the freedom of the unknown in adventures and poems and bring back a report in my little black books.

I took Whitman's words from *Song of Myself* to heart,

> Stop this day and night with me and you shall possess the
> origin of all poems,
> You shall possess the good of the earth and sun—there are
> millions of suns left,
> You shall no longer take things at second or third hand,
> nor look through the eyes of the dead, nor feed on the
> spectres in books,
> You shall not look through my eyes either, nor take things
> from me,
> You shall listen to all sides and filter them from yourself.

16

Plum Nelly

One year my husband and I, both students, spent months searching for a place to live in the country near Urbana, Illinois. We almost rented a house from an old farmer named

Cecil McCormick, but we learned the well sometimes went dry. Cecil called one evening about a friend's house near his on Rural Route 2. Even though it was late at night we couldn't wait to see it. We drove three miles past fields of whirring crickets to shine our headlights on the porch. Even in the dark the place felt right.

The next day we saw that the house had frayed, green shingles, a tin roof, a stand of spruce trees to the north, an old apple tree in back and a wren house on a tall, leaning pole. There were no closets and the plank floors were covered with buckling Masonite. The landlord, Clarence Willms, had run out of wood paneling in the bedroom and finished one wall with bits and pieces. That's how he did things. We began to call this style "Willmsical" after his last name. The house sat on a country acre surrounded by sloping fields raggedy with last year's corn. We began tending the strawberry patch before we moved in.

My friend Martha's mother, Betty, told us the place was plum nelly—plum out of town, nelly in the country. And so that's what we called it, Plum Nelly.

There were baby cardinals in the apple tree that spring, scraggly and brownish. We began bird watching and were even visited by an indigo and a painted bunting. Clarence planted winter wheat around the yard and soybeans in the summer so I wouldn't feel boxed in by tall corn. I enjoyed watching the soybeans sprout, grow and develop fuzzy pods. Sometimes tornadoes passed nearby.

Even though I began to have tornado dreams, I've never loved a home as much. And at Plum Nelly I wrote the first poems that don't embarrass me now. I wrote poems about morning in our yard and about light. I wrote tornado poems. I wrote about Clarence and his wife, Grace. I set a stool in a corner of the yard looking over the field sloping toward the woods and wrote poems about corn and wheat and seeds and crickets. I wrote about my overgrown garden, about an old woman's mirror I bought at a farm sale and about the rickety front porch where we'd sit looking over the neighbor's cornfield.

Places can inspire poetry. To me, a Chicagoan who'd spent years in a beige, brick town house, Plum Nelly seemed like a poem, quirky, lyrical, ancient and fresh with old peonies and roses. It had all the character and mystery of a poem. It had wild chicory and Queen Anne's Lace, a snake in the cellar, old trees and even a weather-worn cemetery up the road. And all this became mine. I knew it, walked it, tended it, planted sunflowers and ferns in it, smelled and tasted it, watched it under snow and wrote about it.

> my house has
> eyes, fields,
> a peak hat, tin roof
> green scales, clover
> birds in the roof,
> squirrels in the attic
> and bugs in the basement, chewing.
> And wrens.

I made this list into a poem, closing with the words,

> and you and I moving through rooms for years
> this house will never remember.

Maybe I loved Plum Nelly because it reminded me of my grandmother's cottage on the Fox River or the Skilles' old farmhouse near

Stone Lake, Wisconsin, where I was happy as a child. Who knows why Plum Nelly felt like poetry to me and may have left someone else cold?

I look for places made of poetry for *me,* places alive with history, wildlife and mystery. Then I move in if I can.

One of my favorite places is a bee-loud glade I've visited in my imagination for years through a poem by William Butler Yeats. I've always especially loved the first verse of "The Lake Isle of Innisfree."

> I will arise and go now, and go to Innisfree
> And a small cabin build there, of clay and wattles made;
> Nine bean rows will I have there, a hive for the honey bee
> And live alone in the bee-loud glade.

PRACTICE

Think of a place that has the mystery or beauty of a poem to you. It might be an old boathouse, a weeping willow, a park you love, a lake, a creek, a sunporch or basement at your grandparents' house stashed with old comic books.

To Andrea a place like a poem was her childhood kitchen when her mother made pithy rhubarb pie and the whole house smelled like burnt sugar. To Danielle it was a plywood fort she made for her sister's eighth birthday when they were kids.

List details that make a place like a poem to you. Use colors, sounds, smells, objects you remember seeing.

Name a place and begin your list. Shut your eyes. Go there. Let the words take you.

17

where do you come from

Bladelike rows of cypress trees along the roadsides in California or in paintings by van Gogh made me nostalgic when I was a child. Though I grew up in Chicago I've never felt Chicago is where I really come from, except for the branches of the mulberry tree or my room in our red brick house, where I dreamed of castles.

My sophomore year in college I went to a Columbia University sailing club meeting. I turned toward the door and glimpsed a handsome sandy-haired young man coming in. In a minute he was sitting next to me, joking with a friend in Greek. I was stunned by his appearance. He looked like one of those classical marble statues of young Greek men you see in museums.

That night I began a romance with Giorgos Marinacos (which means "son of the sea"), an accomplished sailor also turning nineteen. Fresh from Athens, Giorgos was miserable in New York, mistakenly placed in the Columbia School of Engineering, with marginal English skills. He bragged about his life in Greece, telling me his family had a small castle and he sailed with King Constantine. I was skeptical. Our stormy love affair (my first), was on-again off-again until that summer, when we agreed to meet in Athens.

On the ferry to Piraeus, passing the island of Corfu at sunrise, I sensed that *this* was where I came from. I wrote in my journal, "I knew such places had to exist—mysterious dark open light. *Malista* (yes)."

Giorgos was playful, confident and natural in Athens and at his parents' summer house in Monemvasia (meaning "the way to pass through"), a fortress village on a peninsula in the southwest Peloponnese. In winter, water covered the raised road and Monemvasia became an island. Everything Giorgos had told me was true.

In Monemvasia we hung out with the local caretaker, Panayotes, in his sputtering boat, ate with villagers in Miss Matula's cafe, danced the Hassapiko at a midnight fiesta, fished with Labis, who brought us food from his garden, *karpoozi*, watermelon or a knapsack of *aklathi*, hard fresh pears.

It seemed I was meeting Giorgos for the first time. His parents adopted me. Even his gnomelike grandmother said she felt she'd always known me. I sensed I was visiting my past as well as a future where I belonged. Giorgos and I planned to marry and live where I was more at home than I'd imagined possible, in the Marinacos's small turret-topped summer house of stone—close enough to a castle for me—beside a domed church. We used lanterns and candlelight. Two doors faced the sea with ancient cannonballs as doorstops.

In Monemvasia late one night I wrote, "There's a fullness in me and around me *(Karpoozi Uranos Fos)* [watermelon sky light] that nothing but the huge black shadow my leg throws on the church could ever explain." I felt so overwhelmed I added, "I'm in an abyss, as Giorgos would say."

Back in gritty, rushed New York the next winter Giorgos and I broke up. I've never returned to Greece. But recently cousin Harold told me that for centuries my father's maternal family lived somewhere in Greece. Their name, Kallis, means "best" in Greek. I've just found the words "kalos, kalliterros, *kallis*tos"—good, better, *best*—in my journal among other words I learned from Giorgos's mother, Eleni Marinacos, on the balcony in Monemvasia.

PRACTICE

Think back. Where have you felt most at home? Where do you think you really come from?

Sometimes looking at a photo will trigger a memory or a dream even if it's a country or place you've never visited. Collect landscape photos from calendars and magazines. Gather pictures that speak to you: African mud villages, women in saris paddling a boat in India, the blue Ligurian Sea bumping against houses in Portofino, a cafe scene in Miami.

Look for a place in a picture that *feels* like somewhere you've come from—Cornwall or a stone cottage near the moors. Blue snow. The depths of Loch Ness. Begin to write about where you feel you come from.

In an afternoon workshop my friend Ellen wrote with her left hand to tap her right brain (something you might try),

I come from the sky
with all the stars around me.
It's not cold like they say it is.
Shine bright.
The room is blue
and you can rest there. . . .

Landscapes can stir up deep feelings. My colleague Karin Faulkner suggests you first list feelings.

despair joy loneliness fullness confusion silliness
seriousness boredom excitement

and next list landscape-related words,

mountain gully valley hill pebble beach seaside
waves ocean twig leaf anthill desert cactus meadow
fence pool garden creek swamp mud dustdevil. . . .

Combine your feelings with some of the landscape imagery.

Open with "I come from . . ." You might come from mountains of silliness, a swamp of seriousness, a twig of sarcasm, a tornado of anxiety. This will help you see the scenery of the emotional landscape you come from.

In the Juvenile Hall Brian stopped feeling suicidal when he began writing poems. His long poem about where he *comes from* opened,

I am an old one
in the valley of the ancient ones.
I hear their souls talk
in the wind
and I see their faces in the clouds. . . .

18

from my grandmother

•

I remind both my parents of Nanny (Celia Kallis), my father's mother, though my looks are softer, tempered by my mother's genes. Celia was one of the eccentric Kallis women (*expressive,* as my father's cousin Sylvia puts it), but she hid behind her role as a well-to-do Chicago businessman's wife. Her clothes were Celia's only tangible expression of who she really was, along with her severe haircut. She combed her short black hair straight back, accentuating her long face, dark, deepset eyes, widow's peak and aquiline nose. In photos she looks like an elegant, mysterious priestess. To be honest, she also looks a bit like a witch. A *good* witch, I think.

Rows of Nanny's dresses now crush against each other in my closet, a long velvet gown with a bustle, a black velvet coat lined in silver satin, a chiffon dancing dress flaring below the knees, lacy bed jackets, a red robe fit for a countess and wide-brimmed hats with fruit and spangles.

Nanny had a nearly obsessive need for light, for curtains open all the way and for quiet. Whenever I open curtains and follow the sun around the house like a cat and then out onto the front porch with my books, I can hear my mother say, "You're a *Kallis*. You're acting just like Celia." She also says this when I'm bothered by the sound of an air conditioner or the freeway too close to my house.

I remember spending the night with Nanny once in Chicago's opulent Edgewater Beach Hotel. Nanny told me to brush my hair one hundred strokes to bring the oil out of my scalp and make my hair healthy and shiny like hers. I remember touching Nanny's short hair slicked back like a seal's pelt.

That night Nanny wore flannel pajamas with large, pastel polka dots. I still have a swatch of that cloth, the size of a sheet for a doll's bed, I saved from her old pajamas when I found them in my parents' basement.

Once I made a plaster mask of my face and painted a widow's peak on it, mindlessly. The mask looks strikingly like Nanny, as if it were her white death mask, with sequins and sparkles under deepset eyes—mine, black, peering through the holes.

Sometimes I wonder how much I've inherited from relatives. I wonder if Aunt Gert, Aunt Anne and other Kallis women were interested as I am in mystical aspects of Judaism, the Kabbalah, the tree of life and its ten powerful spheres, "the sephirot." My father's great-grandfather was a rabbi in Russia. I wonder if I carry his ways of seeing the world. I wonder what he thought of a rabbi known as the Baal Shem Tov, the founder of Hasidism, who broke rigid conventions and spoke of finding holiness and joy in one's daily life. I've heard similarities often skip a generation. Maybe this is a double skip.

I wish I'd known Nanny's husband, Grandpapa Mitch, a Chicago businessman whose final words were spoken in Choctaw learned from childhood friends in Pontotoc, Oklahoma. At Mitch's deathbed his brother Charlie said, "He's talking Indian talk." Maybe those Choctaw words were the only ones grandpa knew that could begin to take him where he wanted to go.

The mystery of Nanny has inspired me to write about her many times. In a poem recently I realized I was *angry* with Nanny about all she hid and never shared with me and about her unwillingness to discover and be who she really was.

> Nanny, how could you! Wolf, loon
> coyote night diver raven's wing pendulum
> stalk how could you
> wear white gloves to search for dust
> and set no place for yourself at the table.

PRACTICE

Daydream back. Somewhere in your ancestry is a Celtic musician, a slave prisoner, a Druid priest or a Cheyenne Contrary. You may just *sense* it and never know for sure. List the people you *know* are your ancestors, then add other types of people with whom you feel a kinship.

Ask yourself and your family questions. Collect old clippings and photos. Tape them into your journal. Begin piecing together *who* you feel you come from. You might want to focus on one family member who helped form you.

Title a poem with his or her name or relationship—*Poppa, Granny, Ima, Aunt Belle,* etc. Make your poem a letter or a request, whether this person is alive or dead. Ask all the questions you want. Include the answers given back to you if they come. Say everything you've ever wanted to say to this person, angry, loving, sad, confused, accusing or grateful. No one has to read what you write.

Dear . . .
How could you
Why did you
Thank you for
Where were you, etc.

19

lying to tell the truth

My dad always bragged that his father, my grandpapa Mitch, walked barefoot from Pontotoc, Oklahoma, to Chicago, Illinois. There he got a job as office clerk and soon became president of the Armstrong Paint and Varnish Company. Nowadays my dad says it's true his father didn't *like* shoes, but admits he didn't walk to Chicago barefoot; he took the train with his shoes on. My father was making up this barefoot detail. But he wasn't actually lying, he was telling the truth about his feelings of admiration for his father.

Our feelings are often so huge or complicated we can't express them without going beyond normal speech. That is, we can't define them without *lying*. Kenneth Koch points out in *Wishes, Lies and Dreams* that lies belong in poems. It's exaggeration, really, hyperbole, a way of telling an emotional truth. Lying or exaggerating this way gives us freedom to communicate intense emotions.

Of course, I can't lie about the facts. It's important for me to be both real and accurate in poems. First, I have to get the scene and the details right. Is it a *monarch* butterfly or a *swallowtail* I'm describing? Is that a *sycamore* or a *walnut* full of magpies in Kathleen's yard? I need accurate description of what I see to bring the reader with me. Then, with the particulars in place, I can lie all I want to express my feelings. I can be intense and far-out. I can fly, go to the underworld, become blackness itself or a volcano or lace, as long as I'm expressing the emotional truth.

Deep feeling lies at the heart of most good poems. To express her anger and fragility, a senior at Oroville High School named Christi wrote,

> I am a violent whisper
> ready to soar fast as a cat
> black as a thundercloud.
> I hear no laughter only air
> sweeping the ground like a snake.
> Like a diamond I glimmer

but golden and red like a leaf
on a tree I float to the ground
and hit
and break.

Poet Czeslaw Milosz has called poetry "the passionate pursuit of the real." What's real may lie below the surface of fact and we have to stretch the apparent truth to reach it. So, in poems, with the help of lies, we can tell what's real like nowhere else, and sometimes arrive at the emotional truth.

PRACTICE

List feeling words. Creating a feeling wordpool can be a form of incantation to loosen you up to tell big, fat lies.

If one type of feeling keeps coming up, look for the opposite:

disturbed peaceful embarrassed confident bored
secure frazzled together anxious calm excited
expectant
jubilant joyful depressed ecstatic frantic accepted
enraged powerful . . .

Pick a feeling. Use seven or eight word tickets (along with other words) to help you define your feeling. Valerie wrote, *"I feel as nervous as twelve eyelashes."* Sandra, *"I feel as shy as a blind baby."* Word tickets may help you get to the core of your feelings in a way you never could with conventional language.

Let yourself sound crazy. Lie. Blow up your feeling. Make it enormous the way we do when we're hysterical, ecstatic or in the middle of a tantrum, a love affair or a panic attack. You might be amazed at what comes out of you.

Lie, however, to express your emotional truth. Remember the experience behind the feeling, it's tone, color, depth.

Gather some word tickets and begin.

> I feel as disturbed as
>
> as peaceful as
>
> expectant as
>
> enraged as
>
> jubilant as and see where this takes you.

To illustrate the idea of lying to tell the truth in my first workshop session, I often use this poem by a sixth-grader in Mendocino named Gover Tulley. It was published in the 1974 California Poets in the Schools statewide anthology, *I Write What I Want.*

With a
bird
in a
forest
I saw
myself in dog
a pool brown
I saw our
Death black
in a like
glass is
I went mud
to your you
house inside
saw feelings
a are
man poems
named I like
miracles you
I am Like
a mad and I
man flowers
my are
feelings

Notice how Gover's poem grows like a two-stemmed plant out of the word *feelings*.

20

snowflakes and secrets

When I was ten or eleven I caught some snowflakes on my mitten with my friend Loie G. and my unspoken rival, Bonnie, near Loie's squat brick house in our old Chicago neighborhood. I'd *heard* that each snowflake was unique. I'd made flat ones with scissors and folded paper for school walls and windows. But I'd never looked closely at a real snowflake before—a powdery, intricate pinwheel poised like a minicathedral near my thumb.

I called Bonnie and Loie over to see the amazing snowflake on my mitten. Bonnie began to mimick me in a high voice, "Look at the pretty little snowflake!"

I learned that day that there didn't seem to be a place for a person describing a snowflake on a mitten. After that I was quiet about what I saw so I wouldn't make a fool of myself. I learned to be quiet about beauty.

Often we keep secrets because we're not only embarrassed to *be* who we are in front of other people, we feel genuinely embarrassed *by* who we are.

Recently as an icebreaker at an evening gathering I walked around with dozens of adults. We introduced ourselves one-on-one as a favorite childhood game. As a kid I'd pretend I was a horse, a dog or a squirrel. Even my bicycle was a horse I'd water in puddles. So I introduced myself by saying, "Hello, I'm a wild horse, galloping," or, "Hello, I'm a squirrel in a tree," thinking I'd feel okay since everyone was doing this. But other people were saying, "Hello, I'm baseball" or Monopoly, Clue, bingo, checkers or marbles and I thought, Oh, Susan, you've done it again, you've gone too far. You're exposed out there on your squirrely limb, out of bounds. You oddball of oddballs.

In poems we can flourish out there on our limbs. It's one of the mysteries of poetry for me. The language and form of a poem creates a blue bubble I can float into the world as if my secrets are in an impenetrable container with boundaries, yet see-through like a bottle.

I feel safe because poems take me to a place out of normal time and thought, dipping me below the surface to where we all meet. And there, as if we're in silent collusion, it's safe to say whatever we want. Writing poems, we're tapping the part of our consciousness that knows we're safe.

I've seen secret after secret spill out in people's poems, and I've spilled secret after secret about myself. The poem speaks in confidence, the reader feels included, honored, and keeps the secret.

21

listening to our shadow

My favorite book when I was young was *Now We Are Six* by A. A. Milne. My mother tells me I never wanted to turn seven. It seemed like a serious mistake to me. I wasn't eager to become a grownup along with everyone else wearing tie shoes. Before turning seven, I wanted time to stop.

Later I learned that the psychologist Carl Jung suggested (as A. A. Milne and I must have known instinctively) that when we're about seven we separate from and then bury or repress whatever parts of us don't seem to be acceptable in the world around us. According to Jung, these unacceptable parts become our shadow.

If we're shy and withdrawn, it's our shadow who's doing flamenco dances on a table in a nightclub. If we're always doing good turns and being obedient teenagers, it's our shadow who's sneaking out the window at night and coming back muddy and hung over at dawn. If we're rebellious, disobedient and procrastinating, it's our shadow who's on the honor roll.

Laura, with long blond hair, a health food, vegetarian diet and a hand-built house in the pines, discovered that her shadow dresses in tight black leather, wears spike heels, has straight black hair, red lips and black nail polish. She smokes cigarettes through a long, metal cigarette holder. Another friend who dresses in baggy sweats has a persnickety shadow in tailored business suits.

I meet often with my shadow. She's a statuesque Greek goddess who sometimes brings me messages through a cool and unavailable grey cat. I've taken the more boring role of wife, mother and responsible citizen (though my daughter tells me not to worry, I'm weird enough).

To become more fully who we are, it's a good idea to invite our shadow to speak now and then. In the meditation/visualization I practice, I talk with my shadow most evenings about the next day. I'm disorganized and she's a master planner. She knows how to give me free time, which I rarely allow. And I try to spend Thursdays letting her inform me and often take me shopping. She's more extravagant than I am.

Once in Santa Monica she urged me to buy an outrageously expensive ocean green, ripply dress like the one she wears, Greek goddess style. Next door we picked out Grecian-style sandals with leopard straps. She wanted me to wear this to a high school reunion, but I didn't have the courage. Here's a poem I wrote to her shortly after our shopping trip,

My shadow wears
leopard shoes
ocean dress
leopard hat
and she knows
the order of things. Her hair

is green vines
and she lives
to drive men wild,
they walk babbling into the sea.
The mousier I act
the more men she drowns.
My shadow is a grey cat
who makes lizards drop
their frenzied tails
and makes me
wear her
shoes.

Since then my shadow has come closer. I'm listening and we're usually friends. I just shut my eyes and ask her to appear. Sometimes, if I've neglected her, she seems negative or angry until I begin to listen. I ask her what she needs from me. Lately she's been telling me to wear white. She likes me to dance. I need to ask her where and when. Often she wants me to shut doors and get to bed by ten to read. She likes to help me cut my writing. She always reminds me to breathe more deeply. She wants to be on the cover of this book in black, leaping.

Recently my shadow has been asking me to follow her through a rocky valley without looking back. Last week she showed me how to dance a little jig along the way. She's dressed in white herself in what appears to be a bridal gown. I think she wants me to wed her, the disowned half of myself, and begin to experience the unknown: the feeling of being whole.

PRACTICE

Find a quiet place, sit down, shut your eyes and ask your shadow to appear. Your shadow may be angry, weak, sad or frightened because he or she hasn't had a chance for expression. When you bring your shadow to consciousness and begin to meet his or her needs, the figure's appearance will probably change.

Begin a conversation with your shadow. If you're willing, invite him or her to become part of your life.

Describe him or her. Note the changes in appearance as your conversation continues.

Ask what your shadow needs from you to have a positive role in your world.

Where can you meet? What would your shadow like you to do together?

Make a date to meet with your shadow once a week or, if you prefer, every day at a certain time. Let your shadow pick the time and place.

Write all this down.

Let your shadow write a poem.

22

what's my image

•

Poking around the house now and then, I catch myself in the mirror. There's no telling what side of myself I'll see.

One day last week I shifted identities all day. I began as a stereotypical Jewish mother getting my teenagers to school on time. Later I became concerned daughter on the phone with my mother, shifting to shrew in a disagreement with my husband. Talking to Andrea, training to work with poets in the schools, I became a thoughtful mentor, then on to native doing a barefoot samba among overextended women at Give Peace a Dance.

Another evening I rushed into a black Moroccan dress for a costume party. I wore my shadow's leopard shoes, an Indonesian headpiece, ankle bracelet and a huge topaz ring from my mother's friend Ruby. I felt more like myself than I had in years.

All of us play lots of roles and have many sides which come out in different situations. In our writing and sometimes in our lives we can get stuck.

Often in workshops I'll notice someone who writes continually from one persona—the lost soul, the fantasy woman, the Sweet Sue, the angry outsider, the perfect student or the despairing victim. Usually I point out that's just one side or voice. Why not try writing from the opposite perspective? It's always valuable to bring in the opposite writing poems. We may express needs we're not aware we have, coming from parts of us we barely know are there. When counseled to worship the god in him, I've heard that D. H. Lawrence commented, "Well, I'm *many* gods."

At an evening workshop I asked a group of adults to collect different images of themselves—archetypes, voices or ways of being, like clown, fool, sage, sucker, temptress, tyrant, mouse, giant, whiner, Greek god Zeus, Marilyn Monroe, Nazi, weakling, Elvis, Aphrodite, maid, queen, doormat, king, homeless one, judge, wimp, angel, drudge, baby, priest, priestess, convict, rock star . . .

We decided even elements in nature would work: tree, ocean, crow, tornado—whatever seems a part of us and might have a voice. I suggested each person take as many of these voices as he or she wanted—including some opposites, like bitch and angel—and let them speak. In poems there's room for all of who we are, the most seemingly unreconcilable opposites.

Kathy wrote about a paradoxical woman creature "like snowflake obsidian."

In a high school session Matt wrote about the wild party of discordant voices taking place in his brain.

> Insecurity is hiding in the corner. . . .
> Pride is there too,
> arm wrestling with humility. . . .

Rebecca wrote about the romantic, the volcano who rants and raves, the dramatic, the seeker, the griever and the clown who

walks aimlessly through jungles
of overhanging jokes
laughing at nothing.

Phoebe, who loved using the word tickets, discovered some new sides of herself,

I am none of these,
I am not one of the singed or the punctured.
I'm not from here.
I am not from the rustic or cynical.
Cherishing the divine,
always the spicier,
relishing the dances,
pounding on the powdery dust ground,
stamping in the fires. . . .

PRACTICE

List all the sides of yourself you can.

Choose the voices most wanting to speak, including opposites.

Knowing you're the director behind the scenes, encourage these sides of you to go at it, no matter how dark or angry.

Describe what each part of you is wearing, what colors and where that part of you likes to go.

What does that part of you like to eat?

What car does he or she drive? Include details.

Use a variety of verbs: *love hate ask need demand warn advise wear beg shriek sleep . . .*

Two or three parts of you may want to have a debate. Let parts of you take turns—fight, forgive, accuse, confess. Include everything without judging what the different parts of you want to say.

Just write it down.

---

from ALTAZOR

I'm the mad cosmic
Stones plants mountains
Greet me Bees rats
Lions and eagles
Stars twilights dawn
Rivers and jungles all ask me
What's new How you doing?
And while stars and waves have something to say
It's through my mouth they'll say it.

—*Vicente Huidobro*

23

coyote and the wild

A poet needs to keep his wilderness alive inside him.
—Stanley Kunitz

I felt trapped when I lived in Turlock, California. Every inch of land for miles around was either paved or planted and fertilized and sprayed. Only when it rained did the air get the fresh, green smell I needed. I remember sitting in our backyard on Yosemite Street with my two toddlers while my mind flew over rows of back fences trying to find even one native grove of trees. I wanted to leave Turlock partly because I sensed there was no wildness—not a river or stream or lake or even a large park for miles and miles.

I was totally caught up in the role of good wife and mother. It's stifling to be *good* all the time and it's ingrained in most of us. My mother used to end many of our conversations innocently with the words *Be good.*

Always being loving, gentle and good is deadly. I recently heard myself tell a friend, *Don't be too good!* I wish my mother could say that to me. In a way she has. She's always told me all she regrets is what she *hasn't* done, nothing she *has* done.

And it's not my mother's fault that nothing in our middle-class, Chicago Jewish background gave us a sense of the Native American trickster/antihero/animal delinquent coyote who, like poetry, is both naughty and heroic at the same time. To the American Indians, coyote is tricky, magical and often a hero in spite of himself. In one myth, coyote's tail is struck by lightning and as he runs frantically from place to place trying to put the fire out, he brings fire to the native tribes of the world. In a Navajo story, coyote scatters the stars as the elders arrange them on a blanket, fostering the new life that emerges from chaos and disorder.

We all have a troublemaker inside ourselves. Whenever I'm watering flowers out front with the hose I want to spray anyone within range. I almost zapped my neighbor Thurza recently when she emerged from her yard to say hi, dressed for the office. I've learned I can use this impulse in poems. Stanley Kunitz writes, "Perhaps there's too much order in this world"; and like coyote, "the poets love to haul disorder in."

Coyote wants us to be free, to run and howl and play and lope and roll and eat our fill, at least sometimes. There are many wild things to do that don't hurt anyone. Coyote often joins my friend Tanha and me when we're together. Once we draped scraggly grapevines over our heads and shoulders and loped through the park, oblivious to people's stares. Coyote also likes to tell dirty jokes, sneak up on people, shock them and disappear, laughing.

We can live quiet, apparently sedate lives if we express our wildness by risking and leaping in our writing. Wallace Stevens lived an outwardly conventional businessperson's life and wrote poems filled with coyote spirit. "Rabbit light" and "fur light" appear in "A Rabbit as

King of the Ghosts." In his poem "Anecdote of the Prince of Peacocks" Stevens met Berserk in the moonlight and asked him why he was "sun-colored, / As if awake / In the midst of sleep?" This quiet wildness in some of Stevens's poems is like coyote who's there to shock us awake in the midst of *our* sleep.

It's often the coyote in us that gives our poems life. The strangest, most far-out renegade part of ourselves can be expressed in a poem while we sit quietly in our kitchen or bedroom. This can save our lives.

There's nothing appropriate about coyote, nothing dutiful or responsible, and that's why he/she is so important in poems. If we're appropriate or dutiful in our poems, they'll have no spark. Our poems will become predictable, along with our lives, our dreams, our hearts. The coyote in us doesn't give a hoot what anybody thinks. In an early journal I copied down what André Malraux said about the artist Goya, "He discovered his genius the day he dared to give up pleasing others." For me that day hasn't quite come. But I'm inviting coyote into my life more often lately and we'll see what happens.

In her poem "Back to Arcadia," my friend Cassandra Sagan Bell tells how, when she was a child, she blew dandelion seeds all over her neighbors' perfect suburban lawns. "I loved those weeds / with their proud yellow smiles," she writes, closing her poem,

> And me?
> I'm still spreading wild things
> with every breath.

PRACTICE

Let your writing be inspired by the coyote in you.

Find the nearest place you can with wildness in it. Drive if you must, even for an hour. Walk into a thicket or a hollow or a stretch of beach. Let yourself feel part of that wildness.

Write words down. No sentences, no poems, just words.

Let yourself make sounds as you write. Laugh at yourself.

If you can, go out in the rain. Drink rainwater from leaves. Let rainwater fall into your face. Get your hair wet. Write about it.

Let your writing leap. Take risks. In his poem "Father and Son," Kunitz wrote about "the night nailed like an orange to my brow." Coyote made him do it.

The moon belongs with both poetry and coyote. Like coyote, the moon comes out at night and speaks to the wildness in us. Begin to notice and describe the moon—moonrise and moonset. Is the moon a soft ball or a sharp sliver? Is it a cat's eye between cloud lids?

Let your writing surprise you.

Begin your poem with one of these openers,

Coyote and I   or

I am Coyote

Coyote made me

Include the moon. And, sure. Go outside and howl.

24

poems and the body

Sometimes when I swim in the cold creek long enough, I come out a bit dizzy and I like to lie down at the edge of the One Mile pool and peek at the world through the water gathered in my eyelashes. When I squint the drops become prisms. The trees and sky, wobbling through the water, fill with every color.

To reach one of the places poems come from I need to swim underwater, stay up all night or look at things upside down or sideways to tap both my alert, conscious self and my unconscious. I need to delve into my sleep; do and see things from an altered perspective. This not only helps me write poems, it can open up my life.

I sometimes think poems come from electricity in the air, a hum inside, impulses we can feel in our body. When I sense an electrical charge around a person, event or place, I know there's a poem in it, waiting for words. Poems are often about something so important to us we can feel the need to write as a physical urge.

A poem can be triggered by or create a physical sensation. Even reading certain poems can affect our bodies. Emily Dickinson wrote, "If I read a book and it makes my whole body so cold no fire can ever warm me, I know that is poetry." When poet Alicia Ostriker read Sylvia

Plath's book *Ariel,* she responded with "a physical sensation like that of being slapped hard: rush of adrenalin, stunned amazement."

Randall Jarrell wrote that a poet is a person who walks around in thunderstorms waiting to get hit by lightning. In California electrical storms aren't common, so I might have to settle for a flood, an earthquake or at least a long walk in the park and a swim against the current in the creek.

....

All the warm nights
sleep in moonlight

keep letting it
go into you

do this
all your life

do this
you will shine outward
in old age

the moon will think
you are
the moon

—*Swampy Cree*

PRACTICE

Skim these suggestions and try what you want. Read this page upside down.

Stand on your head for as long as possible. Notice details upside down. Look in a mirror. Write.

Dance. Write.

In Squaw Valley at an Art of the Wild conference, Gary Snyder suggested we pad our knees and hands and crawl through the wilderness for a while for a close-up sensory experience of the terrain. Give it a try. Write.

Stay up all night writing poems by candlelight so your rational self falls asleep.

Hang out with a dog, cat, horse or bird. Feel the animal's fur or feathers and let yourself move into creature consciousness. A grasshopper will do. Write from his point of view.

Listen to your breath. Be aware that it's automatic and that breathing, being alive, is effortless. Write a poem about your breathing.

Practice silence. Spend an entire day without speaking. Then write. (I haven't managed this one yet. I look forward to it.)

Write a poem of hunger or food.

Stare at a fire. Let the heat and light fill your body. Write the fire's poem. Toss some writing in the fire. Write about feeling the heat of your words burn.

Notice the weather and write about it. Weather keeps us aware of our bodies, always engaging us with the larger world and bringing us into the present through our skin and breath. Weather is like the earth's breath carried by air into us, connecting us with everything.

Do anything new. It will open you up to feel, see, write and be something new.

25

poems are alive

My daughter Elisabeth's biology class is going to visit a cadaver in a pre-med classroom at Cal State University, Chico. She says she and her friend Emily might stay in a different room and not see it. The cadaver, I imagine, will be cadaverous. I won't go further in my imagining than that. I wish the class would go to a circus instead and watch life pulsing through acrobats and tightrope walkers.

I've heard that when I die my body needs to be left alone for three days. Native wisdom holds that the soul or spirit takes that long to leave fully. After three days I want to be out of sight for good in earth or smoke. This upsets my mother, who tells me Jewish custom is to bury the body *within* three days.

I've noticed there's a spirit or life to moments, celebrations, arguments or lovemaking that hovers around a room, a house or my mind for a while and then just lifts. One day there may be a measurable field of energy for the buzz of life around moments and things.

Poems are alive this way. When a poem comes to me I have to tend it like a small fish, a possum, a snake or a puppy, depending on the poem. It's often kicking and unruly. Most of my poems stay alive for about three days. They can't live without air. If I let too much time pass, the oxygen runs out and the poem may need mouth-to-mouth.

There's a period even after it's written when a poem is alive. If a poem is new enough, it can take off at a poetry reading even if it's not a great poem just because it has that buzz of life. A poem I like better, left sitting too long, may fall flat at a reading if I haven't visited or attended to it. The air around it is too still.

Talk is like that. When I plan what I'm going to say, often the words are strained no matter how brilliant they seemed when I came up with them. They're no longer fresh. It's why I write in the car. If I don't flip that poem onto the page the moment it wants to come out, it can drift away like a dream or go lifeless. Talk is alive. Moments are alive. Poems are made of talk and moments.

Yesterday it poured all day. This morning when I walked Emma down the block, the sun was coming through trees and all the soaked things were steaming. The black trunks of the eucalyptus trees along the drive of the Gonis' five-acre lot for sale were steaming. It seemed that I could see the life of each tree swirling around it in a cloud. The fenceposts were steaming, too, and the black pavement of the street.

I went over and breathed in the steam of a eucalyptus tree. I felt like I was inhaling life force. I wanted my daughter, her friend Emily and the whole biology class to be out there walking too, breathing in the trees.

3

Hi there stars

26

hi there stars

Screaky trumpet, saxophone and flute sounds kept seeping into the room when I held my first poetry workshop at Wakefield School in Turlock, California. I was abandoned in a partitioned area by the music lab with no windows or desks, just folding chairs and a portable blackboard.

Every oddball in the fourth and fifth grades was with me in that class and I felt panicky at first. I read one or two of my poems and told secrets about myself by randomly opening my journals. I read about a college boyfriend named Stevens who wore pajamas under his clothes to save time. I read about how Gail Epstein and I sat in the back of ninth-grade math class counting seconds as we held our breath to build lung capacity. I read a poem I wrote in high school English about watching an elm tree sleeping, listening to the English teacher and hearing "nothing, nothing."

We played with words on the board and talked about where poems come from. We talked about trusting and listening to ourselves. As the ten sessions continued, I was probing, feeling my way in the dark, the way most poems are written. We had good days and bad days when kids wandered off every which way—like poems—and put very few words on paper. I thought, I never want to do *this* again.

Small, wiry Frank seemed to be ringmaster by force of sheer anger and will. He'd bang chairs together and only write standing up—if he wrote at all. One day he wrote an acrostic poem about his name. When he got to the "k" I asked him to include something he *liked* about himself, opposite from the other words he'd chosen. He wrote,

FRANK

•

Forceful
Raging
Angry
Nervous
Kind.

Another day Monica began to explore her idea of who she was.

I used to be a nightmare
but now I am a cloud.
When I sit and look at the sky
I find I'm something more
than just a person.

I began to see that writing poems can help kids shift the way they see themselves, especially if they're feeling sad, walled-off or different from others. In poems, being different is an asset; we don't have to think of ourselves negatively. Our idiosyncrasies are like prizes. We can be proud of who we are. It's freeing to express our one-of-a-kind soul.

Rather than see herself as friendless, Faustina saw herself first as a forest, a tree, and then a leaf, saying,

> Lonely here I ask the wind
> if I can ride on his cool, clear coat.

In these first sessions I began my practice of typing a poem of each kid on three or four pages I'd distribute and later read out loud.

What hooked me on poetry workshops and allowed me to continue was the day kind Frank, skinny, angry and sad as ever, got beyond himself to write about the sky, with a host of trumpets from the music room squawking in the background,

> Once
> I said
> *Hi*
> *there*
> *stars*
> and they were gone.

When he wrote just these ten words Frank shifted the way he saw himself—from troublemaker to potential poet—and overnight his behavior changed. He became a helpful aide, one of the class scribes. That spring we named our class anthology after his poem, *Hi There Stars*.

27

Terra: from dirt to mother earth

Terra didn't write the first day I came to her fourth-grade class years ago. Her teacher told me Terra was dyslexic, with almost no writing skills. When the class talked about names Terra said her name meant *dirt.* Someone had told her this. I explained that her name meant *earth.* Terra was happy to learn that to native peoples she was Terra, mother earth.

We established a pattern. Once the kids began writing each day I'd ask Terra if she were ready and suggest she shut her eyes. What do you see? I'd say, asking her to respond to that day's theme. Terra always saw clearly and knew what she wanted to say, choosing each word carefully. It seemed the poems were waiting in her head. American Indians, Terra was glad to hear, originally didn't write their poems on paper either. They spoke the words the way she did. When we wrote about coyote, Terra dictated,

> I am a coyote running away
> from the spirit of lightning
> and the woods
> saying help me. . . .

I asked if there were anything else. She shut her eyes and added,

I am a butterfly
of sweetness,
of love,
shocking
everybody
with sweetness.

It wasn't hard to see Terra's vision, sense of rhythm and gift with words. In her poem "Moon of Blackness," she dictated,

I see a coyote running
on the moon of the blackness
I see a coyote running
on the star of white.

From an image in one of her poems, Terra took the name *Ocean Water*. Expressing who she was in poems helped Terra shift her perception of herself from a hopeless student and child to a promising poet with the power to move the people around her. I've seen this shift in people of all ages.

A friend editing a Cal State Chico student journal published Terra's poems. Terra and her family were invited to a campus poetry reading. Her mother and father came in proudly along with some siblings, all amazed that Terra was being honored for her writing and that I considered her gifted.

There stood Terra center stage, a star. She listened quietly and with composure as a student read several of her poems to a room full of college folk who clapped and cheered. Maybe this changed Terra.

28

Paul who breaks pencils

In Thermalito last week seventh-grade teacher Bonnie told me it was amazing that Paul wrote two poems our first day. He rarely participated, she explained with exasperation. What he did was break pencils. Bonnie lifted her hands and broke an imaginary pencil in the air. Crack.

Paul, thin with sandy hair, full of mischief, would lean low over his paper in a huddle with the cocky boys at his table, blending in with the wild ones who make noise and give people trouble. Paul was quiet, but his mouth and green eyes were busy. He'd be making faces, almost like Harpo Marx, silently disobedient.

From the list of possible openings that first day, *I am, I will be, I remember, I want, I let go of,* Paul picked *I want*. He wrote,

I want to be the straw
in your cup.
I want to touch
your lips.

The whole class reacted with giggles when we read this. They sensed the slightly out-of-bounds intimacy of Paul's poem, and also experienced the power of the image he created with just fifteen words. A straw is flexible, it can bend without breaking and it can take in nourishment. This is what Paul wants.

For his second, riddlelike poem, Paul chose the lead in *I am*,

> I am a yellow thing
> that people like to use.
> When I am broken in half
> my heart is breaking.
> I am a pencil.

This brittle thing that can be used and that can write but not receive, this is what Paul feels he is. When a friend saw Paul's poem she was amazed at what Paul had done. She said, "Without ten years of therapy he explained why he breaks pencils."

The symbolic language of poems allows us to express and begin to understand not only our feelings, but our idiosyncrasies, problems and fears.

29

the Plains way

Something hampered my decision-making ability when I was a child. I'm often amazed I managed to make decisions that led to having a husband and two children all living in a house on Sierra View Way in Chico. Though indecisiveness may well be part of my nature, my upbringing didn't help. In the Jewish culture everyone is full of advice for others, especially children—telling them what they should do. When we were in Israel, a stranger saw my daughter photographing a windmill at a distance and he yelled, "Stand closer! Stand closer!"

American Indians—at least Plains people, who, paradoxically, value both communality and individuality above almost everything—simply don't tell their children or each other what to do. According to my Osage friend, the poet Duane BigEagle, Plains people may say, "If you don't brush your teeth, you'll get cavities," or, "If you touch the hot stove, you'll get burned," or even more simply, "The stove is hot." But it's up to the child to decide whether or not to touch the stove and accept the consequences. Rarely do the Osage say, "Brush your teeth," or, "Don't touch the stove."

The Osage have such reverence for individuality, Duane says, that even at peril to their own lives they won't tell someone else what to do. If four Osage people are in a car and the driver is heading off the road, all the passengers will say is, "There's the edge!" never, "Don't drive off the road." If they're raised traditionally, Duane adds, they won't even think it.

I decided to practice the Osage way with my family. I'd say calmly to my daughter, "Your sweatshirt is hanging over an open drawer in the bathroom," rather than my normal, "Pick up your sweatshirt in the bathroom *now*." I don't remember whether or not Elisabeth picked up the sweatshirt, but at least I wasn't issuing commands.

For a little while my whole family tried to practice the Osage way. When I slipped into bossiness my son would say, "That's not Osage, Mom." I'd apologize for whining, "Please start studying for your English final!" and correct myself with the words, "The English final is tomorrow, boychik."

The Osage way is like poetry. They both allow individuality. There is no "right way" to do things in the world of poems. And in the process of writing a poem, we go to the place inside ourselves where decisions are made, where who we are is continually emerging and where no one but each of us, alone, can forge the way.

30

I dress myself with rain

I thought I had it all worked out in a workshop session funded by a grant to teach poetry and ecology. I wanted my students to know the names of local plants, animals and landforms to help them connect with their surroundings. I compiled lists of place names in Butte County like Bald Rock, Feather Falls and Table Mountain, along with names of flora and fauna like water ouzel, manzanita, ceanothus, fiddleneck and owls clover. I planned to talk about the watershed and local Maidu Indian words like *talulu* (squirrel), *pompoko* (moon), and *kasa kasa* (blue jay). I was superprepared.

But at Park Avenue—an alternative high school—the students weren't interested in my agenda. They had little patience for the outer world and for names of things. Quotes from famous poets made no impression. They didn't want to hear about Walt Whitman. They wanted to *be* Whitman, and in the spirit of freedom, plunge into writing about the self.

Admiring these freedom fighters, I chucked my agenda, passed around word tickets and let them do whatever they wanted. With photos of landscapes, I *suggested* they write about where they come from, on the inside as well as the outside, so they could write about themselves. But most of them took off on their own.

Erica made long rows of word tickets as if they were a magic pass to her inner ocean. Playing with word tickets, for some people, is almost like discovering a new language to express what can't emerge in normal "talk" or writing. Using the language of the word tickets, Jeremy finally pulled out of his "nobody loves me" mode from earlier sessions and began writing more expansively about how "the patter of rain falls like tears" with the impact as powerful

as the swirls of lightning
the sky's tunnels
hurl at us.

He wrote as if the sky were a person involved in his life.

Aubrey wrote, "I dress myself with rain" as if she were the earth herself, and John, stretching out rows of word tickets, filled his page with images like "Angry hair flows like a river," painting a surrealistic landscape with words showing the connection of our bodies to all of the natural world. These young adults helped me see that by its very nature poetry is a form of deep ecology, allowing us to experience the interdependence of everything on earth.

Poetry and science are different ways of knowing that complement each other. In this workshop I'd been coming from the way of most science, outside in—observing, dissecting, naming. Poems go to the essence of things from the *inside out.* What science tends to take apart, poetry senses and takes in whole. The lily with the bee in the garden. In poems, as in meditation, we can enter the realm plants, animals, words and ideas come from, the archetypal realm of pure mind or imagination where everything is taking form and everything is connected. Kevin, an Oroville High School student, entered this realm when he wrote,

> The world is light with my imagination.
> I feel the stream and let it become my body.
> I drift away from this special place
> like a bug on a leaf.

PRACTICE

> Evening comes bringing all things
> which the bright dawn has scattered.
> You bring the lamb, you bring the goat
> you bring the child to its mother.
>
> —Sappho

My friend Joanne Allred developed a practice where we talk with nature the way Sappho does. Joanne suggests we think of something in nature not just as *you* but as *thou*. Joanne quotes Joseph Campbell in *The Power of Myth*, "The Indians addressed all of life as thou, the trees and stones, everything. You can address anything as thou, and if you do it you can feel the change in your own psychology."

You suddenly sense the sacred in everything on earth, including yourself.

Choose a specific object you normally call "it" and think of it as "thou." Ask questions to help you see its point of view and tap its wisdom. The encounter can take place in your imagination, but ideally in a forest, meadow, field of snow or by the sea or a creek.

You might say, "Oak tree, what can thou tell me about roots and leaves?" Be open to the way the object speaks and every impression you pick up.

....

Know things in nature
are like a person.
Talk to tornadoes;
talk to the thunder,
they are your friends
and will protect you.

—*Anonymous Navajo poem*

31

bring me magic

One spring in a small workshop I suggested we each go outside alone and wander until we noticed an object to bring back to class that might have a quality we needed or with something to tell us. We explored the old car lot next door with weeds coming through cracks in littered cement and a border of maple trees.

"Nothing spoke to me," Stacie said, back inside. Stacie was empty-handed, probably the way she lives. I'd gathered three things, with too many choices, the way I live. I asked Stacie to choose one of my objects and she picked a foxtail seed.

Name it, I suggested, a real or made-up name. Next, describe the seed. *What does it look like?* Compare the seed to something else. Then ask it, *Bring me* a quality the seed has that I need.

I read aloud a few poems from former workshops written this way, as invocations. Seventh-grader Lupe wrote,

> Dead rose,
> crinkly as paper,
> bring me love.

Liou left out the *bring me* part, just naming and comparing,

Rose,
you look like a yellow bell
that hangs from the top of a church.

And Serena,

Leaf
like a red spoon with a thin handle
or a heart balloon on a string,
bring me magic.

In a backyard workshop a woman named Jeri, focusing on "Bring me," wrote,

Striped worn river rock . . .
bring me your heavy wisdom
at the still point in the river
where I can lie back, like you,
in shallow waters. . . .

That spring day at the high school Erica stared at a perfect, round dandelion gone to seed. When Stacie knocked some seeds off, Erica went outside for another. She wanted a perfect sphere. I asked her to look closely, name it and then describe what the dandelion looked like, reminding her that close observation is important in poetry.

Then I asked her to think about a quality of the dandelion that could enrich her life. I felt discouraged and I was pushing her. I asked her to begin, What does it *look like?* What does it look like that it *isn't?* When Erica finally wrote about her dandelion, I was reminded of the power of comparison (or simile and metaphor) to expand our sense of possibility in ourselves and in everyday objects.

Wish dome
it looks like someone shot
an arrow in the moon
or even a golf ball on a green tee.
A domed jungle gym
with small people growing out.
An octopus tarred and feathered.
It smells like starbursts . . .
I can smell the arrow
it flew by so fast.
Bring me the light touch of a bubble
the freedom of air
the firmness and strength of a rock.

PRACTICE

Step outside. If you can't, try this indoors. Take in your surroundings. Look for an object with a quality you need and something to tell you. It may be a natural object, like a twig, seed or stone. It may be man-made like a bottlecap, a knot of string or a bent nail.

In an afternoon workshop an artist friend found an old, broken doll that helped her express her longing for a child and her grief at being childless.

Give your object a real or made-up name. If it's a mushroom, you might call it *white sticky* or *plump cloud.* You might call your object by its real name, *gingko,* or make up *fan leaf.* Write down the name.

Honey mushroom

Next, describe your object by comparing it to something else. You might include where you found it. What does it look like?

Honey mushroom
floating in grass like a plump cloud

Finally, ask the object to bring you a quality it has that you need: the ability to expand or a watery nature or a unique flavor. . . .

Honey mushroom
floating in grass like a plump cloud
bring me your love
of dark places

Find several objects and write a series of short poems in this format:

Name *(real or made up)*
you look like
bring me. . . .

My friend Kathleen Gallo, who developed much of this invocation practice, brings a large roll of butcher paper and crayons or colored pencils. People sketch their objects and write their poems beside the drawing to create a colorful invocation mural.

32

Mojo-squeegie-abacus-del morpho

Slender, with wire-rimmed glasses, a long black coat and the beginnings of a beard, Anthony looks darkly attractive yet shaky, pale and somewhat wasted, the way I picture Proust. We're sitting outside at Chico's Cafe Max and I'm chewing a piece of Tony's gum and then smoking one of his Camels to feel a part of Tony's world even though I don't smoke or chew gum.

It's cold outside Cafe Max, early January with rain on and off. Tony is shaking slightly. He has a delicate yet intense face. I think he's living on coffee and cigarettes. Some of his friends inside are about to resume their ongoing game of chess. There's a large puzzle on a table just indoors through the cafe window.

Tony mentions a Rilke poem with a panther in a cage who takes in an image and swallows it. "It's as if there's a black hole endlessly deep in us," he says. "The image goes so far in it's beyond expression."

"I used to call myself Mojo," Tony says, "*Mojosqueegieabacusdelmorpho*. I *was* Mojo." Tony made up the name with his friends Blue Fish and Roo. They picked the words carefully because of their sound. *Mojo squeegie abacus del morpho*. The name's a miniwordpool. Tony didn't know how to be who he was, Anthony, or to say anything unless it was funny.

We're talking about a poetry workshop where we told kids about lying to tell the truth. Jessica, a student, understood right away that a person might need to call himself a *madman* to express the truth about how he feels.

Tony's more interested in truth. He says, "It's going to be very, very good not lying. Truth was always precious to me. I never lost it, but I had to hide it as a child because I felt it would destroy the things around me. People couldn't take it." I think Tony means they couldn't take who he felt himself to be.

Until recently it was easier for Tony to imagine his death than his life. He'd plan the ceremonies around his death. "I stood in a cemetery with friends in Newcastle," he says, "and decided I'd ask them to gamble away all my possessions, like some Native American tribes do."

"Then I wanted to have my body flattened, dried and pressed into paper, so it could be made into a book of poems I write." Tony lives and breathes poems.

Earlier we talked about poetry belonging to everybody. This excites Tony. He's unhappy (yet intrigued) with the exclusive world of academic poetry. "Poetry's a living art," he insists. "It translates into a way of life. It's song. We sing. It's an act of participation in our world."

"When we listen to a poem," Tony muses, "the world slows down. Poets are the people who listen and teach the world to listen. Talent is important, but the passion is more important than the talent."

Before he wrote poems Anthony didn't know how to share all he has going on inside. "One of the reasons I write," Tony insists, "is that I feel I have so much to say it could *kill* someone. I'd never stop talking." Writing poems, he says, you become a vessel. There's space for someone else to roost inside you. What's inside can be channeled safely out into the world.

Poetry allows Anthony to be who he is. He thinks it has saved him. Once I asked Tony, offhand, if he was going to "do the poet thing." Without hesitating Tony responded, "I *am* the poet thing."

33

skin spinoff

Yesterday Kathleen, Danielle, Beth, Anthony and I were sitting around Kathleen's kitchen table drinking cranberry cider, planning poetry workshops. Mosquitoes wavered around Danielle and I flattened one into her hair as gently as possible. We'd come inside to write.

Outside the February sun was low and seven or eight magpies bobbed on the top branches of a walnut tree. Nearby the orange tree was laden with sweet, solid suns.

Kathleen says I have a knack for opening books to the perfect page and she handed me poet Charles Wright's *Country Music.* I opened to a poem called "Skins." When you're feeling receptive, I think, any page might seem perfect.

Let's write about *skin,* I offered, skin images already peeling through my mind. I'd hit a loaded word, *skin,* a word that can become the core of a poem and trigger a spinoff of every skin memory, skin image and skin association. Not every word is as loaded as skin, but many are. *Wall. Spring. Pretend. Reveal.* The five of us began writing nonstop silently, no discussion or complaints.

Anthony took off playing with sound, naming every type of skin there is—banana skin, coonskin, foreskin . . . Kathleen wrote about her father and brother hunting, with deerskins moldering over rafters. "You can't separate the skin from what it holds," she wrote, "without stopping the heart." Beth and Danielle meandered on their own tangents, unready to read aloud. I wrote about walking above the Dead Sea in Israel, slipping back centuries into reed skins on winter feet, where you hum "so full of night and song your skin can barely hold you in."

As I drove to Berkeley the next day, skin associations continued to pour out and fill a note pad with skin sound, ending, for fun, with

> hard skin on the underside of trembling
> jello cold in the bowl.

This one word, *skin,* was the outer layer of a well of associations that took us each somewhere we didn't even know we wanted to go. I never expected the word *skin* to bring me to a place that seemed like home near Shulamith's waterfall and Qumran in Israel where the Dead Sea Scrolls were found, parchment skin crumbling.

Using one word or idea as a center to return to again and again is a good way to give a poem focus as well as a form and rhythm that gives, takes, breathes and has room (like skin) to expand. This allows us to express our longings, secrets and questions—and to come upon some of our answers.

PRACTICE

Begin looking for words that are loaded.

Begin is a good one. *Window. Door. Mask. Ask.*

Try *skin.*

Take a color. Almost every color will bring a rush of associations. Colors are loaded with memory, smell, feeling, touch and taste.

Notice all the places you see red. A jeep. A red leash, silk dress. Let the colors take you. Write the color's poem. Include foods.

Choose one, *chartreuse, fuchsia, orange, purple, magenta.*

What are all the things that color makes you see?

Yellow

fire hydrants, refrigerator numbers, beeswax, neon letters, calendula, topaz, cat's eyes, fireflies, pencils, squash, yarrow, bees legs fat with pollen, buttercup, bird beak, bellyup sunfish . . .

Write short pieces, one after the other, letting each color move, trigger memories and suggest images, the way I did with yellow.

Yellow sinks
shrinks
floats off, skims past, goes invisible
the closest color to flight
yellow so easily erased by Roethke's mooley slugs
we honor your efforts
to imitate light . . .

go

34

listening in Thermalito

I've just begun five workshops in Thermalito, no-man's-land outside of Oroville, California. There's a rough charm to the ramshackle frame houses where most people can't afford aluminum siding or dual-pane windows. There are no new subdivisions infringing and not much money for asphalt, either. There's a sense of beat-up, renegade freedom about Thermalito and the raggedy open space around it, with an odd mix of olive, oak and palm trees. Most of the houses are on a rise that gets lots of light. Some are the kind of country homes I love.

Yesterday in three classes I met about seventy of Thermalito's fourth-grade children—a number were absent because of torrential rains and flooding. John, the teacher of the first batch, told us a man struck by lightning yesterday was still alive. That's the kind of day it was. One kid told us his house was full of water. The atmosphere was loose and muddy the way I like it.

The kids snapped up odd bits of information I read from my journals. Tomorrow maybe I'll read my new entry about the discovery of a fifteen-thousand-year-old house in the Ukraine made of mammoth bones. Inside the boney house were musical instruments made of *painted* mammoth bones.

I can't help wondering why the world is offering *me* a shot at all the ten- and eleven-year-olds in Thermalito. A flood of fourth-graders. Tomorrow I meet another sixty in two more classes.

I've met Dustin, Shane, Sarah, Kyle, Mai, Sue, Nicole, Kham and Jeff. Like Thermalito's unlikely mix of olive, oak and palm trees, the kids are Laotian, white, Native American—Maidu, Sioux and Cherokee.

I never know when a poem will be given to me, or by whom. An intense redhead named Wayne raised his hand nonstop there was so much poetry in him wanting to pour out. I almost ignored him yesterday, so many hands were going up and we were running out of time.

But I did call on him and Wayne sang for us, words he'd learned from a teacher in beautiful, wobbly alto Cherokee. When Wayne translated the words he brought that mysterious patchwork class into focus, reminding me of the dangers of labeling people, reminding me that poems can bring together opposites and create harmony. Wayne sang, "I am one with the magnificent sun forever forever forever."

I need to take time to listen. It can be an effort to stop what I'm doing and listen to a child, a friend or even to myself.

Writing a poem is a form of listening, helping me discover what's wrong or frightening in my world as well as what delights me. In Thermalito Jessica wrote a poem about a huge black beetle blocking the sun, allowing her to listen to her sadness and let us hear her words.

Immersed in the wordpool, surrounded by word tickets and images on photos and postcards, Hmong children knowing very little English began to write poems from a realm beyond any particular language. Seng wrote about "smelling sunlight," Ellen wrote words like music,

> Paj may
> we we
> wa wa
> lee lee
> rises rises
> moon moon
> sunkissed.

Ki wrote about going to a "truthland"

> where everything is white.
> Birds and deer rush for home.

Brett revealed that, like his Hmong friends, he's a "cloud boy." Then he gave me a folded, paper packet of acorn dust he ground as part of his personal magic in making poems.

And Holly, one of the teachers, took time out to listen to herself and write,

I come from the free light cloud
where it meets the horizon
curving up the ridge
to hold the moon
but only for a moment.

35

misfits' castle of lightning

"I'm tired of people leaving me," Erich told me in the Juvenile Hall. It's my next-to-last visit. I've been working weekly with a small group of young men and women who sleep in tiny cells and live a strictly regulated life. The counselors are trained guards. I watched them dive in and break up a violent fight between Kenny and Conde one day. Pieces of yellow tape on the floor mark boundaries only the staff can cross. Erich is determined to create a world where he'll feel at home and can define his own boundaries.

Nearly eighteen, Erich has been drawing plans, including a futuristic house where he'll live one day with pyramid towers made of windows. "This is my world," he says, going through piles of pictures. "It's the universe I'm creating. I've got to rename the seas. The Gulf of Titania is gonna stay. The Sea of Moons is gonna stay."

Flint questions Erich. "Where are your smaller countries? What about topography? Does it rain? What color is the sky?"

Robert enters in. "What color are the tree leaves? Are there rocks?"

Flint, "Do you have valleys or mountains?"

Staring at an atlas opened to a map of the moon, Erich ignores the questioning. He's entering another realm just by reading and listing names of places he sees listed on the moon: *sea of tranquillity, sea of gold, lake of death, lake of dreams, sea of crises, sea of serenity, marsh of decay, sea of rains, foaming sea, sea of fertility, sea of nectar, seething bay, bay of rainbows, ocean of storms, marsh of sleep.*

Flint has labeled the Juvenile Hall "the misfits castle of lightning." Eager to re-create his life, he writes, "Too bad life is written in pen. If it were written in pencil we could erase our mistakes and try again."

Like Erich, Flint and John have begun creating an imaginary world where they name the seas, rivers, mountains and valleys. They're looking at maps for ideas. Right up in northern Washington within a map-inch of Spokane there's *Tum Tum, Bluestem, Dishman, Opportunity, Mica, Spangle, Waverly* and *Inchelium.* In Australia there are the wonderful-sounding *Taree, Toowoomba, Wagga Wagga* and *Wangarralla,* along with *Goondiwindi* and *Dubbo.*

In love with sound as well as the meaning of place names on the moon, Erich begins a poem about where he needs to travel to learn what he needs to know. . . .

From the sea of tranquillity
to the sea of serenity
across the marsh of decay
to the sea of rains. . . .

PRACTICE

. . . there never was a world for her
Except the one she sang and singing, made.
—Wallace Stevens

Find an atlas and look at some maps.

Make a list of place names you like.

Begin to imagine a planet or a country or an island where you'd like to live.

Begin to paint this place with words.

What color is the sky? Are there rocks, hills, mountains?

Name the landforms.

Are there trees? What do they look like? Describe and name the flowers.

Place yourself there. What does the ground feel like under your feet?

What kind of person, or being, could you allow yourself to be there?

36

please don't understand

Oh to be delivered from the rational into
the realm of pure song.
—Theodore Roethke

Recently I worked with a group of women, a few in their teens, who have substance abuse problems. Some, on their way in or out of prison, have had children taken away by Children's Protective Services.

The wordpools these women generated reflected their experience,

wicked shoe day jim jam alienated rainbow
minute wait whirlwind kicken chicken
princess singular ravaged empty full angry
hurtful healing Dodge Dart Plymouth Duster
Buick Skylark exhausted hyper energetic confused
guilty innocent suspicious trusting trapped red jealous
blue secure ankle diamond street percentage stretch
running.

One woman named Jenny had a hard time with the wordpool.

"Don't start with me first. Don't put that down! Don't start," she'd say, wanting to shut down the process.

When I asked, "If you were a shape, what shape would you be, what sound, what number, what song?" Jenny insisted "I don't *understand.*" Even when she wrote a bit and closed a short poem with "I am the ocean," she insisted she didn't understand. I tried to explain that she didn't need to understand. Does the ocean, or you, or I, always need to understand?

People often say they don't understand poetry. It makes no sense to them. Poetry sometimes takes us not into nonsense, but *beyond* sense. I told Jenny and her group, Don't *think*. Forget about understanding. Write down what you *see*. Look down. *Toe.*

White moth blackbird low cloud. Spill words out in pairs, then threes, then fours. This creates a rhythm. Please *don't* understand. *Redwing blackbirds. Cow fence. Stop ahead.*

Pretend you're a wolf, writing.

You're a coyote, a crow, the Fool himself. You're a two-year-old dictating images a machine turns into words. You're a newborn baby with a tape recorder translating images into words with no built-in critic. You're tossing in sensory impressions. They're raw.

According to poet Robert Bly, the Chinese believe that in ancient times, when inspired, the poet flew from one world (or part of the psyche) to another, riding on a dragon, leaving long trails of dragon smoke.

Poet Marianne Moore wanted more than to ride a dragon with a tail of smoke, she wanted to be a dragon. In her poem, "O To Be a Dragon," she wrote,

my wish . . . O to be a dragon
a symbol of the power of heaven—of silkworm
size or immense; at times invisible.
Felicitous phenomenon!

Bly urges us to return to the mysterious world of dragons. Talking about form and technique, he argues, throws light on writing poetry, but light is the last thing we need, he says, quoting St. John of the Cross, "If a man wants to be sure of his road he must close his eyes and walk in the dark."

Rumi wrote,

I want
to say words that flame
as I say them,
but I keep quiet and don't try
to make both worlds fit in one mouthful.

4

Open the window

37

open the window

In the 1970s my husband, Kent, and I drove a U-Haul we named Boris from Illinois to the San Joaquin valley town of Turlock, California, where we were moving, sight unseen. Turlock is famous for its turkeys and the college—where Kent had a job in the math department—is nicknamed "Turkey Tech." I'd been prepared for a desert like Kuwait, but Turlock was green and farmy, though it smelled strange and was known for a mysterious malady having to do with poultry droppings called "valley fever."

We rented a bungalow full of built-ins on Florence Street. I no longer had a job, but I rented some pasture. Then I bought an unmanageable horse named Smokey. Soon we found an unmanageable shaggy dog named Willy (Sweet William). Within three years we also had a son, Daniel, a daughter, Elisabeth, and our own chartreuse house on 1033 Yosemite Street—all unmanageable.

When my children were born I stopped writing poems. I kept my journal to record feelings and what my kids began to say, but not much else. I was so busy being a mother I felt like I was underwater. I wandered around our house as if it were a yellow submarine without enough air.

When my son was a toddler, to help survive the loss of a manageable private life, I joined a small writing group. We named ourselves the "Bag Ladies" and met every week or two to talk about our writing.

One summer morning I was driving toward downtown Turlock when I realized I was baking in the heat. I couldn't breathe. Watching a wasp go limp at the windshield, I came to my senses and thought, *Open the window*. I rolled down both windows in front and let the hot wind blow across me.

The words "open the window" kept rolling around in my mind. *Window* comes from the Scandinavian "wind's eye." I never consciously said, "This is a metaphor that means something for my whole life." But when I got home, "Open the Window" came pouring out of me for days. This wasn't Susan trying to be a poet. This was Susan being informed relentlessly by her unconscious.

So many parts of me weren't being expressed in my roles of wife and mother in Turlock that my unconscious was literally shrieking for more freedom. I began writing page after page in the same rhythm, pulling in everything around me, caught in the experience as if I were in a trance pummeled with images about opening, loosening, letting in wind, cats, geese, day, night, blackness, light. Catching all this and writing it down seemed like a matter of life or death,

Open the window
the mummy's behind me
the sheets are all twisted
the knots are untying
loosen them, cut them
and open the sashes
the moon in the window
the night is now passing
blackness, the blackness
I must let it in
the cat and the wasp and the night
and the wind. . . .

Though I wasn't consciously unhappy, I wrote a poem within the poem called "For Virginia Woolf." I felt I understood from the inside out why Virginia drowned herself.

"Open the Window" came along to show me I was in emotional trouble and helped me express it. Writing the poem was enough. I wasn't going to stop being a mother. For the time being, Turlock was our town. But I did begin moving out into the world, giving poetry workshops and taking art classes.

When I read some of "Open the Window" to my Bag Ladies writing group I wasn't sure it was a poem. It seemed like a waking dream I was narrating, an outburst to help me breathe and expand. Jerry Newman, a visiting novelist from Vancouver, Canada, said, "If this isn't a poem, what do you think it is, chopped liver?"

The poet Paul Carroll wrote about being "ambushed by a poem." That's what it felt like at times, as if the poem were in charge, rushing through my body. I was just a pawn with a pen, taking it all down. So in another poem I asked playfully that all this stop.

The muse *did* leave, as I'd asked, and then I missed the flood of words and inspiration. It's never come to me quite like that again with such intensity for so many days. Maybe that's because I've never been underwater for so long since then or lived in such a state of self-imposed limitation. But when inspiration does come in a rush of energy or a word or phrase surfaces, like "open the window," I pay attention and write.

PRACTICE

Where do you need freedom in your life? What part of you is longing to be expressed that you've ignored (or shut off) for fear of failure, fear of success, no time, or because you're being overly responsible?

Ask that part of you to speak.

Have plenty of paper available. You may experience a flood the way I did.

38

stirring the sky

Each child is born a poet and every poet is a child.
—Piri Thomas

When I saw my son, Daniel, shaking our new lilac bush the spring he was three, I managed to keep myself from shrieking, *"Stop it,* you're going to kill the bush!" Instead I asked him what he was doing. "I'm stirring the sky, Mama," he told me. I asked only that he stir it gently. How can you tell a child to stop stirring the sky?

For years I recorded my children's words in my journal. This helped me *listen* and ask my kids questions rather than simply tell them to stop. It also helped me see how close we are to the source of poetry when we just begin to talk. My daughter, Elisabeth, called a tunnel in the park *wormtight.* She made up the word *slurming* for the way snails move. More recently she coined *ruggling* for wrestle/snuggling. One day, digging with what he called "the too sharp knife," my son explained, "I'm fountaining dirt."

Listening to my children has kept me from always being a know-it-all. Mothers love to make pronouncements. When Daniel asked me what was the darkest color, I knowingly answered, "Black." He thought about this for a minute, certain it couldn't be so simple. Then he said, "A hundred times purple is darker than black."

Children naturally see and express things in a fresh way before we teach them the "right" way. When my children were little they said things like "I have hands," amazed by the discovery. They were filled with questions, "What would happen if the moon burned?" or, "Can a fire burn a fire?" or, "Do bees pee?" or, "Are plants afraid of scissors?" and, "Do roots have minds?"

Poetry can bring me to the child-place where I begin to ask this kind of question, where I begin to discover the world all over again. Hanging out with children helps. Poet Kenneth Patchen wrote that a poet should "wear comfortable shoes and see a lot of children." Poet Francisco X. Alarcón writes,

> A poem
>
> makes us see
> everything
> for the first time.

This is what listening to children can do.

When my son, Daniel, was three or four he had an argument on the telephone with his friend Per. I jotted down what I caught of his end of the conversation, and now he gets royalties (two dollars) whenever I read it as a "found poem" in my workshops.

Bye bye anything I've ever seen computer
bye bye you dirty ball point banana
Bye bye poison fly
bye bye flea of soda pop
Oh you plum,
you fly in a spider's web,
This is making me mad, mad, mad!
Why did you say shhhh?
Want a kiss?
Did you hear it?

PRACTICE

Seek out children. Jot down what they say.

We can find poems just by listening, being a scribe and catching the words.

39

who were you in my dream?

For several summers my husband and I rented a small house on the Oregon coast near Newport for a few days. It's homey. There's a huge window to the ocean and a stickery, slick path with ropes, planks and banana slugs that finally dropped us down on Highway 101, where we zoomed across to the beach. We had lots of evening time there with puzzles and no phone or TV.

One night I began asking my kids questions from one of my workshops. We were making poems out of the answers. My daughter, Elisabeth, said she'd much rather write poems than read them. I think most people feel this way. We started with the questions I've used in a small writing group on my back deck in Chico:

> Who were you in my dream?
> What were you eating?
> Why were you hiding?
> What were you wearing?
> Who was with you?

Making up questions became as much fun as answering them. We'd begun intermingling our dream world with what was around us. Asking someone, "Who were you in my dream?" invites that person into contact with our inner world. We begin to see that happenings or people in our dreams may have a correspondence in the outside, or "real" world. This helps the conscious and unconscious meet. Poems naturally emerge from this meeting.

My kids fell right into the mood when I began reading the questions. After I asked her what she saw *in my dream,* Elisabeth answered,

The slanted walls
the echoing water
My mom told me never to fear.
The grass was calling
to the monster's hands.
Lovingly the sky held me. . . .

To *who were you in my dream* my son, Daniel, began, *I was the digital firefly,* and then, to what were you doing, *I sold you suction cups.* To what did you hear? *The music was my sustenance, only less yellow.*

Both my kids plunged in. The dreamy mood made Elisabeth see shapes in the ceiling plaster from her top bunk.

I see a penguin, a mermaid,
a koala in scuba gear
and a whale swimming on the walls
to join in the molding.

Daniel asked, *Where did they come from?* "They come from the plastering man's tool," Elisabeth said, "smoothed out softly."

D: *What did they need?*

E: Endless flowers.

D: *But, what did they WANT?*

E: Plummeting rainbows.

D: *How did they get it?*

E: Pens and pencils writing slowly.

PRACTICE

For this practice you can try asking the questions of yourself, but you might want to work with a writing partner or in a small group. If there are two of you, interview each other and record the response to each question like a reporter.

You can alternate, asking each of you one question at a time, or ask one of you all the questions first.

In a small group either divide into pairs or ask questions in a circle, recording answers and continually inventing more questions.

Who were you in my dream?
What did you hear?
What were you wearing?
What were you eating?
What did you want?
Why were you hiding?
Who was with you?
Where were you going?

See if your answers or your questions begin to seem like a poem. Take all this as far as it wants to go.

40
collage

The question is not what you look at,
but what you see.
—Thoreau

This morning I dreamed I was following my mother down rickety stairs into a historical museum. After admiring the Shaker tables, we discovered stashes of my old toys as well as my children's. There was the red vinyl fire engine my son and daughter used to push across the yard, veering past the heather and the orange tree. There was Elisabeth's small, wooden duck on wheels. Mom and I began to pull treasures from under tables, leaving a trail on the floor—my old acorn sculptures, clothes and scarves and pearls as well as toys.

My mother went to get the car, leaving me in the deep, old rooms—the basement, I think, and the attic of myself—where the content of poems is waiting to be pulled from dreams and boxes, glued down and rearranged.

In New York City last summer I discovered Charles Simic's book

Dimestore Alchemy: The Art of Joseph Cornell. For a long time Simic wanted to "make poems from bits of language," the way Cornell made collage boxes out of bits of stuff he collected on the streets of New York. In his prose poem, "Secrets," Simic writes about Emily Dickinson and Cornell, "If her poems are like his boxes, a place where secrets are kept, his boxes are like her poems, the place of unlikely things coming together."

The word *poem* comes from the Greek *poein,* to make. In a collage, as in many poems, you reassemble fragments of found or collected images to make a new image of your own.

Cornell believed that you don't make art, you *find* it, accepting everything around you as material. Artist Kurt Schwitters, a contemporary of Cornell's, collected scraps of conversations, newspaper clippings, tickets and stamps for his collages and poems. Both T. S. Eliot and Ezra Pound thought of their poems *The Waste Land* and *Cantos* as collage.

These artists and poets wanted to remove the separation between art and life in our culture.

Recently I saw a display of collage boxes by a local artist that seemed to define her inner world in images. The boxes contained broken pieces of mirror, a marble, a goblet, a small gold cat, leafy earrings, a wasp's nest, wooden beads, a long bone, quails' eggs, a spoon, weeds and nuts painted silver, bits of broken china, foil and candles.

I pinned an old wooden box full of butterfly wings once, dozens that drifted below the butterfly plant (buddleia) on the back deck. I hung the box in a show with a word ticket, "A little sad."

At a party in Berkeley last Saturday an artist named Nancy displayed two sculptures she pieced together from the remains of her house that burned down in the Oakland hills. The base of one piece was a blue ceramic menorah her son made. In place of candles Nancy stuck her mother's silver-plated knives. Three blackened blades stood like dark flames on one side of the menorah, three scorched handles on the other side. A deck of old gin rummy cards sat in the middle, ace of spades up, indicating the luck of the draw in what survived the flames.

The collage could have been a poem with each found object a word or phrase symbolizing light, survival, freedom and fire, collected and assembled to create beauty out of loss.

Greek poet George Seferis wrote that "To say what you want to say you must create another language and nourish it for years with what you have loved, with what you have lost, with what you will never find again."

PRACTICE

You might find bits of poems anywhere around you—in a cookbook, on a menu, or even in your local telephone book in the *L*'s: *LaFever, LaFlamme, LaFleur, LeGrandeur.* Jane's friend Steve loves the juxtapositions in the headings at the top of the Yellow Pages, *Divorce-Dog. Elevator-Embossing. Marble-Marine. Market-Marriage.*

When I hand out postcards in workshops I often suggest that people flip the painting side over and steal snatches of the messages for their poems. Anthony used Deborah's phrase, "I haven't been able to communicate very well, / but I have been able to sleep."

It's fun to make collage poems and paste things in, literally and figuratively. Andrea and I helped kids make "I am" collages to illustrate poems about themselves. Recently Andrea traced kids' bodies on paper. They glued images representing parts of themselves all over their paper heads, hearts and feet—Mona Lisa, a squirrel, stampeding horses, a baby blowing bubbles and a night fountain with blue reflections.

Make an *I Am* collage. Cut out colors, pictures and words that help define you. Gather stuff from your house, yard or street. Glue it onto cardboard or into your journal in a minicollage. You can also use any box you find or make out of wood or cardboard. Put whatever you want inside—tickets, stamps, magazine clippings, cut-out words. Draw and write in it too.

Write the words your collage would say if it were a radio or a narrator. Jot down the poem of the collage. Let any object in it speak. Let the parts argue, compete or woo each other.

Then hang the collage or give it away.

41

the center of the house

My father used to smoke a pipe he filled from a squat, brown-and-green ceramic tobacco pot. It sat on an end table by his winter chair near the fireplace. If I could have become that jar, I would have been witness to the secret of our lives in the red brick house of my childhood, 8201 Champlain, on the south side of Chicago. I might have seen my mother pacing, uneasy in a neighborhood she was happy to leave. I might have heard the click of my door when I went to hide or the creaking stairs as my brother Richard dashed up and down, up and down.

My dreams often take place in that house. Maybe that's because for me the center of the house was my bed, where I first began remembering dreams. Each night I'd leap into bed from a distance so whatever the bed hid underneath couldn't grab me. Then I'd stare at the squares of pink and blue and white on the wallpaper, making each color take its turn as the corner in a pattern. I'd watch the stain shaped like a ballet slipper for a while and then shut my eyes and pretend I was a squirrel foraging in the woods. Sometimes, eyes shut, I'd watch tiny dots of color moving out like an infinite field of bubblegum balls.

One day, sitting on the covered, clanking radiator next to my bed, watching our sour cherry tree, a winter sparrow and the garage roof with turrets like a castle, I decided to imprint *that moment* into my mind forever. I willed myself to remember the image of the sparrow and roof and tree as a connection to my unknown future, which, of course, is now. It worked. I remember.

That's the center of my house for me, the area in and by my bed where I dreamed myself into being—not the fireplace, not the kitchen with the cold tile floor and not the tiny room where my family gathered off the kitchen. It was my dream center, my bed, where I let my mind wander, dreamed of flying and began to imagine who and what I might become.

PRACTICE

It can be easier to write about the center of our houses than the center of ourselves, yet the process can take us to the same place.

Shut your eyes and fall back. Enter your childhood house and wander through. Where do you find yourself wanting to go? What seems like the center of the house? Is it the bathtub where you scrubbed and floated and soaked? Is it the kitchen, or your bed?

Include smells, colors, sounds and comparisons. What do you hear people saying? You could begin with the line,

> In the center of the house, I . . .
>
> I see

I hear
I smell
I . . . (whatever you do)

Use specific, concrete details. Pretend to be an object in the center of your house—the staircase, a chair, a rug or a plant—and see what impressions you receive.

42

grocery weeping

I've just been shopping with my mother, Ethel, in Mr. G's Grocery in Chicago, not the store in which she's most likely to weep. The store that usually gets her crying is the Hyde Park Coop with its labyrinthine aisles that dead end, its soaps where you'd expect pasta, and lines that form when you try to leave even the produce section, where each cucumber has to be priced and weighed like a gold nugget.

I thought my mother was an isolated case. But when I told my friend Martha about Ethel's grocery store weeping episodes she told me she also weeps or comes close in the supermarket. Martha says everything *comes together* in the grocery store. "It's where you have to choose between your time and your money, between skinless and skinned, or one ply and two ply." Martha asks her husband, Larry, for half a Valium before they shop because she can't "go in cold."

I thought it must be pure coincidence that I know two reasonably well-adjusted people who weep buying groceries. Rows of food soothe me. But I'm thrown for a loop in malls and department stores, where I suddenly think I need Aztec print beach towels, 350 thread-count Charisma cotton sheets, nubby bathroom rugs, suede running shoes, silk underwear—and that's just the beginning. I don't get weepy. I begin to dart between sections, depressed about my frayed towels, and sometimes I have to leave fast, deserting an Aztec bath mat in the men's underwear section.

Today I mentioned grocery weeping to my friend Barbara in Sacramento, expecting her to laugh. Instead, she yelled, "Oh yes! I sat on the floor in the grocery store once because I couldn't decide what to buy. It was Sunday night. I was alone and I'd broken up with Ralph. I wanted to buy yogurt, but I knew the grape yogurt wouldn't be good for me. But it was the hair stuff that sent me over. I thought, maybe my hair's not the right color. Maybe we'd have stayed together if my hair was blonder. But red hair was becoming fashionable too. I'd been playing tennis all day and I was tired. You know what weirdos are in the grocery store on a Sunday night, nobody but losers. So you feel like a loser. I had the whole week in front of me and no food. I sat on the floor by the hair color and cried. I left without buying anything and got Mexican take-out on the way home."

Last week on the way to Sacramento one evening I drove through

Oroville, a melancholy town in broad daylight. In moonlight the place made me feel like weeping. What really got me were the lit-up rows of storage rentals on the edge of town. There was a vacant village filled with what we fear to lose, lumpy remnants of lives we've moved away from but won't relinquish. We fill boxes and lock them in silent cubicles resembling motels for the dead, lit up like an advertisement for abandonment. Then we drive past them alone at night and nearly stop breathing.

There's a storage unit poem in me, and a grocery weeping poem about being overwhelmed by stuff in Barbara, Ethel and Martha. And though I'm more likely to find poems in what brings me joy—waves of birds flying over Lonestar Road, the Sacramento River and the Princeton Ferry—I see that my most recent beginning of a poem is melancholy. I compare the fading moon in the electric arms of the oak to an approaching car with one headlight going dim. Padiddle. That's how I was feeling about my lackluster life right then.

PRACTICE

Think back. What was your state of mind yesterday at 3:00 (A.M. or P.M.)?

What was your main mood your junior year of high school?

What triggered your state of mind when you woke up this morning?

What triggered the mood you're in right now?

Begin to corner a mood or state of mind by describing exactly whatever thing, person, place or situation triggers it. If you can give us the details, colors, sounds, maybe you'll trigger that state in us. Maybe we'll experience it, too, and you won't be so alone with it.

Your mood might have been triggered by an overstocked bookstore, a fluorescent waiting room, your neighbor knocking at the door, a night cat crying or a phone call from the attendance office at your teenager's high school.

Write down all the details.

43

joywriting

Walking through Berkeley on an overcast morning recently, my friend Jane and I passed a front yard with alyssum tumbling onto the sidewalk along with purple salvia and other flowers in colorful bunches floating among rounded rocks. We found ourselves feeling happy. Later, we had a sinking spell when we walked by a barren, rubbly yard with cigarette stubs and gum wrappers strewn about. We talked about how we're affected by the looks of a place and we wondered if other people react this way to what has been nurtured or neglected.

When I was depressed in the New York City winter, I wrote very few poems. I remember jotting in my journal, "Citied, bottled, cubed, I dance in a soda glass. I grab for a bubble, boom!" There wasn't much more poetry in me than that. Occasionally writing a poem can pull me out of depression by helping me express it.

I'm most satisfied with the poems I've written from a joyful state of being. Joy as I see it involves embracing life. This can include moments of sadness, grief or rage as well as happiness, unlike depression—where feelings are cut off. I've always remembered a quote from Teilhard de Chardin I saw framed in my friend Mona's meditation/ironing room in Turlock, "Joy is the most infallible test of the presence of god." Our itinerant rabbi in Chico, Stephen Fisdel, says the Kabbalah teaches that true worship of the divine comes through serene joy. Joy isn't the opposite of sorrow, but encompasses and transcends sorrow. You know you're truly connected with yourself when you're experiencing joy.

I guess I like my poems best when they emerge, if not from joy, from engagement with my surroundings. A poem written this way can be as nourishing as a waterfall.

Last week on the back deck I was visited by a mockingbird singing his form of poetry. For all the world the mockingbird sounded like he was flying from treetop to telephone pole, playing with bird words—their rhythm, speed and modulation—purely for the fun of it.

The poet Keats, I read in the *Oxford Book of Literary Anecdotes*, was less interested in his finished poems than in the state of joy he felt writing them. According to a friend of his, Keats often left his finished poems on scraps of paper lying here and there. "He cared so little for them himself when once, as it appeared to me, his imagination was released from their influence, that it required a friend at hand to preserve them." His friend followed Keats around, salvaging these scraps. On one he found and rescued the famous "Ode to a Nightingale."

In her poem "The Stone of Heaven," Jane Hirshfield writes, "Any woodthrush shows it—he sings, / not to fill the world, but because he is filled."

44

the image angel

Things hidden rap at the doors.
—Ukrainian proverb

In a class I took once poet George Keithley said the word *image* in Syriac (ancient Syrian) means both icon and angel. An image, he explained, is also an angel—a messenger moving between the physical world and the divine. Through images we enter the imagination, a doorway to the divine.

Images often appear as messages from the unconscious, especially in dreams or daydreams. Sometimes important images appear in the real world, right in front of our faces. We need to pay attention to images that arise. This doesn't mean analyze them to death. We can follow them to see where they lead our writing and our lives.

As I sit here staring out the window, a scrub jay flies down to the lid of the redwood hot tub outside and takes off with a marble. What an image! The marbles are up there in a box beside the cat's Science Diet in a pie tin. Now the jay dips into the marbles again, but I'm not sure what he's stealing. Here he comes, dashing in blue. This time I see it clearly. He's flapping right over me with a translucent blue marble.

I'm so glad I was watching. How many messages do we miss? I never could have made up such a great image. A blue jay flying over my window with a stolen blue marble.

Maybe the jay's lining a nest with round blue marble windows, letting in blue light to shine on small eggs. Surely this nest is glowing blue, woven with leaves, sticks and grasses. I'd love to live in a round house with blue windows in the top branches of a liquid amber tree.

Now I realize I was being visited by what I call the image angel. She came to me while I was driving through the Sierra Nevada foothills to Lake Tahoe. She made me see that every image around me was speaking to me about the nature of the world and my place in it. I began to see that the images she brings me—slow traffic, spiders' eggs, a man dressed in a map of the world—are messages to connect me to the world outside.

I wrote a long poem about the image angel in the car on the way to Lake Tahoe, beginning, "Sometimes she's the hawk / on top of an oak / or a fencepost trailing barbed wire," and going on to say,

She's been a tornado
and a dustdevil talking to itself.
A sunset once, she took me
dipping below my place on earth. . . .

I learned that the image angel is around all the time if I'll just *notice,*

She may be the saint with merciful eyes
or the snake I must step on to understand
skin.
And she wants to take me with her
huge and slow
in a glacier scraping land
into pebbly lakes
or short-lived
in lightning
snapping along the world
and my spine.

Shortly after I discovered the image angel I held a workshop in the tiny farming town of Orland. It was one of those mornings when I felt I wanted to quit my poetry sessions. There were too many students. I wasn't going deep enough. Besides, I thought, *this work doesn't really reach anyone. I impose it on people. This is unnatural and a waste of time.*

When I got to the large, hot classroom in Orland I told everyone about the image angel. There were rows of faces in front of me, all silent. There was Selina trying not to care; Rikki, whose poems indicate a grim life and a lush imagination; Tiffany coming alive with words. I could tell they understood what I was talking about, as if the image angel were a familiar imaginary friend bringing pictures they needed to see. Even the teacher seemed comfortable with the idea. I began to feel at home. My doubts fell away. Maybe the image angel painted angelic rows of faces in class that day to help me out. Seventh-graders don't always look angelic.

The image angel, I think, is an aspect of the muse. She brings me images from the outside, while the muse helps me see and listen within myself.

PRACTICE

Everything in this world has a hidden meaning. . . . Men, animals, trees, stars, they are all hieroglyphics. When you see them you do not understand them. You think they are really men, animals, trees, stars. It is only years later that you understand.

—Nikos Kazantzakis

What has the image angel placed in front of and around you? Say there's a teapot on your desk—cobalt blue elephants painted on a white porcelain sphere with a spout and a handle. See the teapot, for now, as a messenger, an angel, bringing you information from another realm. First describe what you see. Then jot down what the image angel is telling you through the teapot, sofa or the photograph of a veranda in Greece.

What is he or she seeking to reveal or uncover?

In what way are your surroundings (the objects you choose and see) informing you?

Think about what's around you that you've *bought*. Think about what you've *found* and what's been *given* to you. Imagine each thing is a disguised angel with a message from a hidden part of yourself.

When ants wander into your kitchen see ant as image angel.

Take a walk and for this once see each object, each person, each tree, as a messenger. Describe whatever catches your eye.

Allow a message to surface. It may be as simple as *look at the world*. Notice. Be here. Engage with nature and your neighbors. See the whole scene as part of yourself, speaking to you—if only for this once.

45

the great Magus

Visiting my parents in Chicago one evening, my brother Richard's family sat down with me and my kids to play the dictionary game. A rotating player finds an obscure word like *balbriggan*. Each player makes up a definition. The reader recites all the definitions—including the real one. For balbriggan it's *knitted, unbleached, cotton underwear fabric*. Players win points if they guess the word's true meaning and more points if they fool others into choosing their made-up definition.

The dictionary game folded, but my nephew Andy began exploring words. First he found *williwaw*, meaning "a violent gust of cold land air, or a violent wind, agitation or commotion." I just learned that *Williwaw* is the title of Gore Vidal's first novel, and that his most recent book is called *Palimpsest*, which means a text written over an earlier text that was erased, with a few traces showing.

A word like *williwaw* or *palimpsest*—suggesting faraway places and times—can trigger a novel or inspire a poem. I wonder if the word *palimpsest* spurred Galway Kinnell to write,

The poem too
is a palimpsest, streaked
with erasures, smelling
of departure and burnt stone.

I told Andy about the word *havasu,* which means "sky-water" in both Navajo and Turkish. *Havasu* is like a poem in itself, suggesting clouds, fogs, hurricanes, mist, steam, geysers, waterfalls and breath.

In the living room in Chicago that evening Andy started reading words he found near *williwaw: wimple, willy nilly, wilton,* creating his own small wordpool.

In his poem "Rooms," Lucien Stryk tells how he'd "read through the dictionary, stalking new words for verse" to create "a poem heavy with maypops, fruit of the passionflower."

And in his "Ode to the Dictionary," Pablo Neruda calls the book "the great Magus." He writes that he ignored the dictionary in his arrogant youth but later saw it rise up as a guide, a marvelous apple tree, and words "quivered brightly in its inexhaustible canopy of leaves, / words opaque and musical, / fertile in the foliage of language, / laden with truth and sound." He spoke of the dictionary as a "field of rubies" with a "thousand hands" and a "thousand emeralds," a place with "dense, musical jungle depths. . . ."

The dictionary is an enormous, alphabetical wordpool filled with hidden beginnings of poems. It's a magical place to *discover* words, not just to look up their meanings. I've seen kids in workshops practically fight over the dictionary when it's used this way.

46

controlled abandon

I tell you: one must have chaos in one, to give birth to a dancing star. I tell you: you still have chaos in you.
—Nietzsche

We all need rooms (or teepees, caves or castles) that won't let in the rain, cups to hold water or soup, pots, envelopes, bean bags. Sentences (though I frequently abandon them) for ideas. We need parentheses. Bodies. Words. Our skin and bones and body create a structure and vehicle for the expression of our minds and hearts.

I was talking with my friend Buck recently about a concept that's always interested me, the idea of *controlled abandon*. Among everything else mysterious that a poem is, a poem is a place where chaos can play. A poem is like a stage with curtains, wood floor and maybe even an audience, where words can tumble and loop freely in a Möbius strip—infinity.

A poem can provide a form for the expression of the unconscious or whatever we want to call the voice that comes out of us sometimes, near sleep, in sleep, in the car or through our fingers and thumbs at the keyboard or the drum.

People don't expect poems to be logical. Lightning might strike on any line. Content and form can be turned upside down, as in a surrealistic painting with the stars and clouds meandering inside a house and curtains suspended in the night sky. But all this sky is contained in a frame.

It's a paradox that structure brings freedom. A desk, an empty room, a piece of lined paper, these forms have enormous potential. The universe moving through us needs a mooring. For me, the structure of marriage brings freedom. But freedom for one person can be bondage to another.

I like the idea of controlled abandon. In sex this might be tantra. In poetry it's form. Yeats said that a finished poem "made a noise like the click of the lid on a perfectly made box," implying that a poem *is* a box or vessel with a definite shape. When it's finished it can be closed.

Last night the poet Kim Addonizio said she'd been writing sonnets and spent a whole summer thinking in iambic pentameter (ten syllables to every line, with every other syllable accented). She's been reading the poet Molly Peacock, who likes to write in structured forms to balance the content of poems she calls "out there."

Hart Crane thought the poet's fundamental tasks are "unbound thinking" and "bringing the immediate world into form." He thought a writer must be "drenched in words, literally soaked with them, to have the right ones form themselves into the proper pattern at the right moment."

Along with the forms we intuitively give a poem in free verse—the form of most modern poetry—there are many named forms for poems, including prose poems, sestinas, haiku, villanelles, cinquains, rondeaux and pantoums. I like to create my own forms and rhythms to see where they take me.

A simple way to play with form is in an acrostic poem, where a word is written down the page and each line begins with that letter. In one of my first workshops, quiet, angry Kathy wrote,

Red is for
Entering
Dumb poems.

Kathy was calling both her poem and herself dumb. With a little encouragement she changed just one word from dumb to delicate. Within the structure of a poem Kathy began to shift how she saw and labeled herself,

Red is for
Entering
Delicate poems.

Kathy's poem is only six words. It's like a corridor. The spareness allows us to enter and experience the delicacy.

In the garden my yellow coreopsis look best when I cut the dead heads and even the wilting blooms. The same goes for my writing, which often comes in floods. The dandelions, the poke, the sticky weed, the Bermuda grass, all have to go. Well, maybe not the dandelions.

Before I cut I often have to push a poem. When I heard poet Robert Hass read once, I kept thinking he'd finished and then he'd nudge the poem further. As Hass read "My Mother's Nipples" (and the title's a stretch in itself), I noticed him drawing us again and again into a new direction. This pushing is necessary because poems are vehicles to take us somewhere new.

Though occasionally a poem comes out whole, most poems need rewriting. Poet Lucien Stryk said, "I like returning to a poem and making something of it, discovering that I've been given another chance." Donald Hall claims he wrote 150 drafts of his poem "Henyard Round."

Many poems need to be cropped. Often I cut more than half of what I write—words, phrases and whole sections. Cutting is part of controlled abandon. It's one of the most critical aspects of writing and shaping poems. After pushing, I have to let go of my words as freely as I toss them into the wordpool, especially adjectives and adverbs. I delete *beautiful, and, really, that* and replace *flowers* with *hyacinths.*

Opening and closing lines are most important, as well as first and final words. The first and last few lines in my poems usually have to go. And as I cut I need to decide where my lines break, influencing the rhythm, leaving space to breathe. Also the right title can provide a new slant and dimension or give a poem closure.

Just because I've written minute details and described a moment doesn't mean I've found the poem or reached what matters most to me. I often have to push, cut, push, cut, and still a poem will only take off when it has heart.

In an essay on Charles Wright called "The Nothing That Is," Helen Vendler describes "the voice of the body . . . the voice of the mind . . ."

and "the voice of the soul." She writes, "None of these voices is interesting to poetry, of course, unless the heart is present, too."

Some poems need to be left untouched, just as they emerge. The Zen attitude is "first thought, best thought." When we do cut and polish, we need to be sure our words stay alive and keep their heart. Stanley Kunitz says,"Part of the freshness of the poem comes from leaving some of that primordial dew on it, not polishing the language down to the point where it becomes something made, not something born."

A writer named Marilyn read her poems to a group in Chico Monday night. For over a year she's been writing a poem a day. It's become part of her meditative practice. She's not concerned about putting structure in her poems as much as about putting structure in her life by writing poems.

For several years my friend Lew has written daily "moment studies." He limits his observations to postcard length and sometimes, he says, "a poem happens."

Not only can a poem give form and expression—controlled abandon—to the chaos in us, but writing poems can bring structure and meaning to the sometimes chaotic days of our lives.

Here's a short poem I wrote a few years ago, showing the changes I made on one of the drafts.

...

Early draft

MY SEA RECORDS

Crustaceans, ~~soft seaworn purple~~
~~spines~~
sandworn
~~of the sea~~ urchin spines
sponges,
bristly rocks,
~~sea~~ anemones,
bottles with messages.
Now we're getting warmer,
closer to ~~the deep~~ sea ~~heart,~~ bottom
the green sea turtle,
migrations, the pull of ~~the~~ tides,
and
my wildest dreams
curled
on ~~a small,~~ damp paper
in a bottle wearing ~~thinner~~
Thin,
rolling toward shore,

...

Later draft

SEA MESSAGES

Crustaceans
sandworn urchin spines
sponges
bristly rocks
anemones
bottles with messages.
Now we're getting warmer
closer to sea bottom
the green sea turtle
migrations, the pull of tides
and my wildest dreams
curled
on damp paper
in a bottle wearing
thin, rolling
toward shore

PRACTICE

Try putting only one, two, three or four words on a line. You're more likely to use words you really want. Pick a strong first word for a line and a strong last word. Soon you might find you have only strong words in your poems and not so many *ands*, *ifs* or *buts*.

My colleague Cecelia calls skinny poems spine poems. Write one like the vertebrae in a spinal column. Just toss words down

one
or two
to a
line

Try a haiku. Buy a book on poetic forms and write a sestina, a villanelle, a sonnet and a pantoum. Read poems in books and magazines and begin to notice their form. Copy them.

Create your own forms. Write a line with two words or syllables, then three, then four. Repeat this pattern or any other.

Create an acrostic by writing a word down the page. Use words that begin with the first letter on each line. Make the poem relate to or define the word that stretches down the page.

Only ink
Curling . . .
T
O
P
U
S

A POET IS A RIVER

a poet
is a river

flowing
unnoticed

caressing
the stones

moving
silt from

one place
to another

carving
mountains

all the way
to the sea

a poet
is a puff

of fresh air
in any room

a poet
is a mirror

a clenched
fist

a bleeding
nose

a poet
is a smile

laughter
and tears

a poet
becomes

a table
a guitar

a house
el barrio

speaks
in tongues

brings back
the dead

makes
possible

the fields
the mountains

—*Francisco X. Alarcón*

47

poem sound and song

I hear drums. My son and his friend Anthony are jamming in the shed. They call themselves *Booty Mookie*—both words mean bad. Recently they made a tape called *Taco Loco*. They love language and sound. Other local bands play with sound and sense in their names—*Electric Circus, Spark and Cinder, Road Rockets, Fandango, Laser Bean* and *Los Franciscos*.

Many poems are written for the ear and fall somewhere between music and talk. We come from an oral tradition where poems were sung or chanted, and this is still all around us, "powerful as living breath," insists Abenaki native poet Joseph Bruchac. "Sometimes what seems most fragile catches the most light."

Chants in particular have a repetitive rhythm with repeated words that can put people into a heightened or mesmerized state. Words tossed out rhythmically even in a wordpool can move us into a near trance when we get caught up in the sound, as in the Plains Indian dream song attributed to a Teton Sioux named Siyaki,

> At night may I roam,
> Against the winds may I roam

At night may I roam,
When the owl is hooting may I roam.

At dawn may I roam,
Against the winds may I roam,
At dawn may I roam,
When the crow is calling may I roam.

Poet Stanley Kunitz has said that "few young poets . . . [are] testing their poems against the ear. They're writing for the page, and the page, let me tell you, is a cold bed." As a child in Massachusetts, Kunitz swam in Webster Lake, which he learned local Indians called "Lake Chaug-gog-agog-man-chaug-ga-gog-cha-bun-agung-amaugg." This means *I fish on my side you fish on your side nobody fishes in the middle.* Kunitz writes, "I suppose it is in the nature of the poet, beginning in childhood, to love the sounds of language. Others may swim in Webster Lake, but poets swim in Lake Chauggogagogmanchauggagogchabunagungamaugg."

In native poetry words are called, sung or chanted, often by a priest or shaman, to affect both the individual and the universe through the power of the sound and rhythm of the words as well as their meaning.

We all have an individual rhythm in our breathing, our heartbeat, our walk, talk and even in our thoughts that's expressed in our poems. Even modern poems written in free verse have a rhythm and a pace. We use our instinct and ear. We break our lines where we want to hear a pause or take a breath. The poet Charles Olson wrote, "And the line comes (I swear it) from the breath, from the breathing of the man who writes, at the moment that he writes."

One extra word can ruin the sound of a line. Sometimes a line just needs another syllable to sound right. *Shoe.* Or the poem might sound best with an *o* sound, *mow,* or two *e*'s in a certain place, *seaweed.* The poem might need more silence around it in the form of white space.

Alliteration—*fifty fiddlers feuding*—might create a desired effect. The same is true of onomatopoeia, when words imitate what they describe—*buzz, hum, cuckoo, chickadee.*

Sometimes I wake up with words in my head, and often sound is more important than sense. One morning I woke up saying words that imitate the sound of rowing with squeaky oars, "Speak H, speak H, speak H, / the slow sound of oars."

Poet Sandra McPherson says many of her poems are influenced by listening to blues. Charles Wright is known to listen to country music as he writes. Many poets cite jazz as a source. Music can bring up images and often it seems we can actually *see* the sound.

Once when my toddler daughter was humming, my son, Daniel, asked her to stop. He said the tune made him see hearts and he hated hearts, especially the sharp red poke at the end. Images are triggered by the feelings and memories the music conveys. In a workshop once, a young student named Cody drew images to music and labeled them: *dancing ghosts, insects band* and *singing volcano—low voice.*

Some poets work from sound. They may not even care what the words are saying. The sound can evoke images and meaning to express a more primal experience, as in Charles Wright's poem #12 from *Bloodlines* that opens, "Oval oval oval oval push pull push pull. . . ."

PRACTICE

Make up a string of words because you like their sound. *Awilawona hawoon fazool . . .*

Put your words together in a nonsense poem of sound. Notice what colors, shapes and images these sounds make you see.

In a workshop once my friend Leslie Kirk Campbell asked us to list sounds that seem sacred:

bird song, tree frogs, lullabies, bells, cats purring . . .

list sounds that seem profane:

lawnmower, blowers, garbage trucks . . .

list sounds coming from things that normally don't have a sound:

orange, moon, frailty, sunset, sunrise, dusk, earring, bee sting, fear . . .

Weave images from these lists into a poem of sounds, repeating lines and words to create a simple rhythm.

48

abracadabra

When we lived in small, flat Turlock, California, I'd imagine and dream of a town that suited me more, a smallish, green college town near wilderness, with water and sun on rocks. My husband's sabbatical brought us to Chico, a place I'd barely heard of on the edge of the Sierra Nevada foothills, a green oasis with creeks running through and with sun on rocks. We stayed. Most of my life dreams and wishes have come true this way after a time.

When I care enough about myself I wish not only for things, but for a way of life and a way of being. So often we shrink our dreams and expectations to a small, dank room of desire with no windows, not to mention doors. I think what we dream or wish for ourselves, no matter how limited, is usually what we get. We're told not to be greedy. We don't want to be disappointed. "Don't get your hopes up!" we've heard many times. "Be realistic."

Poetry takes us to a realm where it's possible both to discover what we deeply wish for and begin to imagine it, the first step in making it happen.

In *The Wishingbone Cycle,* Jacob Nibengenesabe, a Swampy

Cree poet, reminds us of the importance of wording wishes carefully, since we often get exactly what we ask for. We must choose each word carefully.

> There was a storm once.
> That's when I wished myself
> into a turtle
> but I meant on land!
> The one that carries a hard tent
> on his back.
> I didn't want to be floating!

He closes his poem,

> I've got to wish things exactly!
> That's the way it is
> from now on.

In *The Way to Rainy Mountain,* Native American poet Scott Momaday says that nothing comes into being until there are the *words.* We need to honor words, be aware of them, let them loose to lead us. The words we use inside and out—for thought and speech—come largely from subconscious associations.

A documentary on China reported that writing was created as a form of divination, a way to connect with, hear from and channel the divine. In Chinese, my colleague Peter Chou tells me, the word for poetry, *shih,* is composed of *yen*—word or language—and *szu*—temple or monastery. "In Chinese," Peter says, "poetry is a temple of words."

According to ancient Hebrew wisdom, sounds, or words, produce reality. Letters and words are elemental creative forces central to making things happen. In his *Book of Letters,* Rabbi Lawrence Kushner explains that Hebrew letters are holy in themselves and are vessels that contain the "illumination of the boundless one."

To students of the Jewish mystical book of wisdom, the Kabbalah, *letters* are creative elements, and *words* that combine and direct the force of the letters are a primal energy force. In *Genesis* it's written that light was brought into being by means of the utterance "Let there be light."

Abracadabra, the seemingly nonsense word we invoke in magic tricks, comes from Aramaic, the language of the Bible: *abraq ad habra.* These ancient words mean "I will create as I speak."

We can't go idly about wishing this or that without understanding the power of our words. The idea that poems or words don't make things happen is laughable to Native Americans who believe that stories, poems and words are alive and powerful.

Lately I've felt hesitant to make wishes. Newly in awe of the power of words, now I most often ask for the highest good, whatever that may be.

BIRD TRACKS ON WHITE BARK

Ishi, a Yahi,
loved matches,
how easily they strike fire.
Words on paper
have no apparent glow.
Ishi called them bird tracks on white bark.
But words on white paper
can move from mind to mind
like flames from roof to roof in wind
not one word spoken.

—S.W.

5

Lights and Mysteries

49

the ginkgo

Why, who makes much of a miracle? Not me!
I know nothing else but miracles!
—Walt Whitman

It's nearly fall again. Our neighbor's huge female ginkgo tree was scheduled to be sawed down today. Every fall she's been producing more stink bombs. That's what we call the wrinkly, noxious-smelling fruit that drops for months in thick piles on the back deck and the path into the side yard where we keep our bikes. All year I've tried to think of solutions, like hanging nets to catch the pale fruit before it spreads its odor into our yard and house. I wanted the tree to know we loved her but my family of bike riders couldn't tolerate her nasty-smelling fruit.

Even with vigilant raking the fruit squishes under our shoes and into our bike pedals all autumn. On hot days it bakes in heaps and the putrid smell hangs over our yard, a nearly visible brown orange ginkgo smog. Last year there were tens of thousands of stink bombs. Flaky mounds still disintegrate under the tree and bushes nearby. Tiny ginkgos wave from our compost, the edges of the house and from the deep flower box where I shoveled reeking loads under the potting soil before I planted snapdragons and foxglove.

Here it is, chainsaw D-day, and amazingly the tree has *no* bombs! Maybe the ginkgo needed a rest after last year. Maybe over the winter she went through ginkgo menopause to become a crone. After all, she's approaching fifty. Maybe she's been reading our thoughts and she outsmarted us. After canceling the tree crew, our neighbor Tom stared up at the fruitless tree today and said, "It's a miracle."

Ginkgos are known as living fossils, the only remaining species of a tree group widespread in prehistoric days. They're sacred in the Orient, preserved from extinction in Buddhist temples. The healing properties of the leaves and nuts, long treasured in Chinese medicine as an elixir of youth, are now being studied in the West.

Now that the ginkgo has been spared, my son, Daniel, and I can see a branch over our roof holding ten or twenty small fruits. Daniel says, "We can't expect her to be *perfect.*" When I commented that the ginkgo must have known what was going to happen, Daniel remarked, "She'd have to be pretty dumb not to catch on."

Our experience with the ginkgo is in the realm of the great mystery, the unspeakable—what poems are often about. My friend Tom Centolella named his new book of poems *Lights and Mysteries* after reading the Baal Shem Tov's words in *Tales of the Hasidic Masters,* "Alas the world is full of enormous lights and mysteries but man shuts them from himself with one small hand."

We need to write about what we know, but we must also be open to the mysteries—rain, light, air, fire, trees, babies, ourselves. In poems we gather mystery, explore mystery and create mystery. Poems are not a place to try to explain things. "Every writer finds a new entrance into the mystery," Chinese poet Lu Chi wrote in A.D. 261, "and it is difficult to explain."

Poems hold the invisible. Clues. Fingerprints. We come upon evidence in images—of apples, ginkgos, torn shorts, clouds, steel wings, a woman's hair in a tight, black bun held with thin pins.

50

Home Song

When my mother's mother, Rosel Frank, was in her nineties she lived in the Self-Help Home in Chicago created by Jewish refugees from Germany. Many of her friends from the old neighborhood were there. I remember seeing them years ago on the grey wooden steps and rickety back porches of Rosel's old apartment on University Avenue, where she'd shake out the dust rag, hang clothes and kibbitz with Hansel Levi, Paula Baer and Emma Fisher. In the communal life of the old apartment (that smelled always of my grandpa Theodore's cigars), Rosel was known for her shrewd card playing.

When she first moved to the Self-Help Home Rosel played a mean game of canasta or gin rummy with Harry Fisher and other old neighborhood friends. But when she turned ninety-four her condition deteriorated, and though still in decent health, Rosel was moved to the dreaded "seventh floor," where everyone knew that self-help and gin rummy were no longer possible. Rosel became despondent.

One morning a few months after my grandmother's move, I sat on the bed in my daughter Elisabeth's room in Chico. Something compelled me right then to write a poem to Rosel, or G.G.—for Great-Grandma—as my kids called her. I chose Elisabeth's room because of morning light. Early sun streams through two windows, casting small blue-and-green squares on the walls from a stained-glass piece she made in school.

I wrote a simple poem in this morning cathedral and then a melody came to mind. I found myself singing what I called "Home Song" to Rosel.

> Oh lord the quiet
> beyond the quiet
> my pale cocoon lord
> so slow the weaving
>
> I've known dark tunnels
> with roaring traffic
> now I need rain lord
> so soft and windblown,
> my lord so warm light
> I'm coming home.
>
> Lie down in sweet grass
> breathe deep the tanned earth
> my home the forest
> my home the sea. . . .

The next evening Rosel died in her sleep.

My friend Rob tells me that in Viking times every man was expected to be a poet. If a captured Viking could compose and recite a skillful poem to please a rival king, the Viking's life might be spared. To be slain in battle composing a poem recognizing the valor of your opponent was considered the most honorable way for a Viking to die. Rob remembers reading these words in an Icelandic saga, *"I see your bright sword / is sharp today / home to my heart it comes."*

Poems are needed at times of passage like birth, marriage and death. Like candles and psalms, poems not only help celebrate or clarify, but they can open or ease the way.

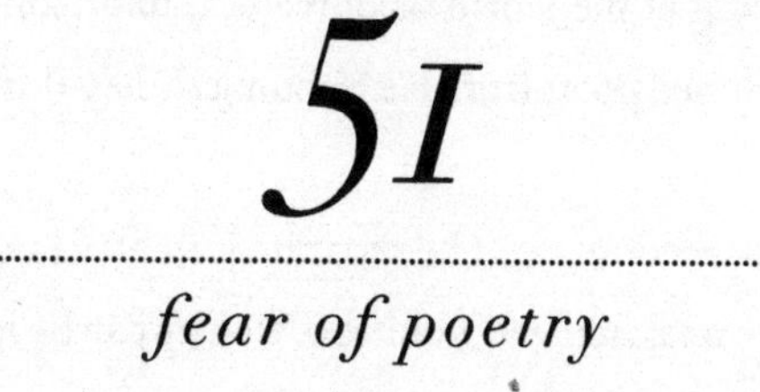

51

fear of poetry

Yesterday morning my friend Arielle told me she was afraid of bats and moths. "The rhythm of their flight is very erratic and hysterical," she said. "And a moth's body is this chunky, awful thing. But it's mostly the flight that's so disturbing."

I guess I'm afraid of bats too when they fly near me at dusk in our yard. And I don't like those slow, dusty moths, either. I wonder if people also fear poems because of their erratic flight? There's no telling where a chunky or thin poem will land. And poems can take *us* places we might be afraid to go.

We fear poetry, I think, for the same reason we fear rainforests, the depths of the ocean and our own unconscious. We fear the unknown, particularly inside ourselves.

My friend Mary Ann told me once about a lizard trapped in a room where she was housesitting. She couldn't rescue the lizard because it was afraid of her, so it died, hiding from its source of freedom. This made Mary Ann think that often what we fear the most might be what frees us.

We tend to mistrust our own natures, as if uncontrolled we'd be freaky, dangerous, hateful, unacceptable or at best, dull. I think in our culture we fear wisdom. For centuries we've stifled ideas that threaten our way of looking at the world or ourselves, imprisoning or burning heretics. Plato banned poets from his Republic. They threatened his idea of civilization.

Poetry and freedom can't be separated. Poetry takes us places we might never have imagined we would go. Poetry can be incendiary, revolutionary, outside bounds and rules and systems. Poetry is uncontainable and, therefore, dangerous, ignoring the established order.

Poetry may change our idea of who we are, and certainly other people's ideas of who we are. In the process of writing poems, *who* we are may actually begin to change.

In his book *Remembering Poets,* Donald Hall argues that poetry attempts "psychic revolution, not to overthrow reason, but to add old or irrational elements to the light of consciousness by means of language." Poetry exists, Hall thinks, "to extend human consciousness, to bring materials and insights from the unconscious dark into the light of language."

Poems can disturb us when we read them and especially when we write them. Poems can also thrill and expand us. They can speak for us in ways we never knew we could speak for ourselves.

IN WHITE AMERICA

1

i come to read them poems,
a fancy trick i do
like juggling with balls of light,
i stand, a dark spinner,
in the grange hall,
in the library, in the
smaller conference room,
and toss and catch as if by magic,
my eyes bright, my mouth smiling
my singed hands burning

—*Lucille Clifton*

52

dreamsense

Last night I dreamed I had a new baby, only it was an egg, small and robin's-egg blue. Everything was in disorder in the house as I tried to protect and nurture my egg on the corner of our velvet love seat. I was holding it against me, afraid it would break. A few minutes later I dreamed my baby bear was ranging about the house. It was small and cute but a little wild, and I thought, "What if it grows into a grizzly?"

A few nights earlier I dreamed that after I dusted cobwebs out of a large, sandy cave, Jackie Kennedy Onassis was there serving me potato salad and bread on an ornate silver platter. She was wearing a black pillbox hat and a skirt so tight it was hard for her to bend. I remember wishing I'd taken more bread.

Poems and dreams come from the same symbol-full well of the unconscious and they often make the same kind of sense in the trappings of nonsense. My friend Mark Rodriguez calls this *dreamsense,* a word for poetic intuition or the sixth sense. It's like discovering a new land, Mark says. When you start tapping dream consciousness you enter an inner realm where you can explore a terrain almost as real as the outer landscape. We tap into this landscape in meditation, in dreams, and we can dive into it when we write poems.

Words sometimes spill out of my daydreams when I'm driving or walking. And I like to write at night or early morning, collecting phrases from near sleep, like,

> the ocean pulled the wind along
> with magnetic breath

Magnetic breath. I write this down in wobbly sleep-writing. It's dreamsense, the knowing that comes out of nowhere, it seems, or from dreams. In Paradise, fifth-grader Michael wrote,

> The path is an enchanted, glowing mudstream.
> To enter, you must have dreamsense.

Using the other five senses grounds us in the here and now and helps us feel and describe place in poems. Dreamsense provides entrance to the collective unconscious, Michael's "enchanted, glowing mudstream."

Sometimes I wake up with words like,

> I've lived in this town a long time
> and last night the best thing for me
> and my honey to do
> was pick fireballs out of the wash.

If my notebook's by my bed, I catch these words from dreams. Often other words start coming until I have a poem. "Fireballs" went on for pages. It came early one morning when the light was slipping through misting rain, and I allowed words to fill me, images of rain and buckets and a proper tea party at my mother's with a glinty green stegosaurus the size of my thumb living in the basement. I suspect many of us are visited by such words and images that fade like dreams as we wake up.

When I tap dreamsense, awake or asleep, I'm writing from an altered state of mind, often a waking dream that comes with a message from a less accessible part of my consciousness. Writing like this is a form of receiving. Again, I need to be *present.* I keep paper and pen on hand and try to catch the words that come and take the time to follow them.

PRACTICE

My friend Barbara says she likes to "gestalt" her dreams, following the theory that every person and thing that appears in one of our dreams represents a part of ourselves with a message.

Begin recording your dreams.

Write several short versions of a dream in which you take turns as the central players. First write what it feels like to be the dog in the dream. What is the dog learning or experiencing? Next write what it feels like to be the car in the dream, then the house, etc.

If there are people in the dream, take turns writing about what it feels like to be them. Write the dream briefly from each point of view.

If the dream is a nightmare, rewrite it with a happy ending.

Let one or all of these versions of your dream turn into a poem.

WRITING IN THE DARK

It's not difficult.
Anyway, it's necessary.

Wait till morning, and you'll forget.
And who knows if morning will come.

Fumble for the light,
and you'll be
stark awake, but the vision
will be fading, slipping
out of reach.

You must have paper at hand,
a felt-tip pen, ballpoints don't always flow,
pencil points tend to break. There's nothing
shameful in that much prudence: those are our tools.

Never mind about crossing your t's, dotting your i's—
but take care not to cover
one word with the next. Practice will reveal
how one hand instinctively comes to the aid of the other

to keep each line
clear of the next.

Keep writing in the dark:
a record of the night, or
words that pulled you from the depths of unknowing,
words that flew through your mind, strange birds
crying their urgency with human voices,

or opened
as flowers of a tree that blooms
only once in a lifetime:

words that may have the power
to make the sun rise again.

—*Denise Levertov*

53

being visited by words

A poem-drenched state of mind, where poems start coming to me even in my sleep, can be invited or induced. In groups I've seen this spread from person to person. It can be contagious, a kind of contact poetry high. In one group, after we created a wordpool and read some poems, a young woman named Angel shut her eyes, tipped her head up and let words flood in. Then she'd record a poem as if she only had to *allow* it.

It's possible to deliberately tap your unconscious. Norman Mailer says you have to be "married to your unconscious" to write. State a problem and suggest to your unconscious, "I'll meet you there tomorrow." Amy Lowell would drop a subject for a poem into her mind "much as one drops a letter into a mailbox." She'd wait for an answer to come "by return post" and eventually the words of a poem on a given subject would form in her head.

Milton wrote about his "Celestial Patroness who . . . unimplored . . . dictates to me my unpremeditated verse." Words came to poet Hart Crane in dreams. He felt as if he were "dancing on dynamite." He could see his entire poem "The Bridge" in his mind and said he was able to jump from one section to another like a "girder-jack hearing the absolute music in the air."

A kind of poem-fever is most likely to come over me in the car when I'm alone and driving fast somewhere far. This is where I write more of my poems than I like to admit. Coffee or tea helps. But I have to be open, have paper and pen and watch where I'm going rather than what I'm writing. I've written a whole series of love poems to Lonestar road—a ten-mile stretch on the drive from Chico to Berkeley. My first one ended,

> . . . Lonestar,
> you lie still
> for your rushed lovers:
> road runner, tumbleweed
> shadow of crow, fall morning
> haze, and me.

Often when I'm driving I begin feeling I'm a part of what I see and write about. I want to *join* the redtail hawk scanning the roadside, *be* the wild mustard floating over Lonestar Road. "I'm spring with lambs in my fields," writes fourth-grader Danielle. When we write poems this way, with metaphor, metamorphosis can take place. Susan and oak. Susan *is* oak. Susan *is* hawk. Yo, I'm the mustard!

In the early morning this state also comes over me now and then, often when it's raining. During some of my wildest moments nothing happens visibly but I'm being visited by words. One wet March I wrote, "Before dawn when I'm immersed in words, the poems are given to me in the dark. Lines chat in my ear or move across my eyes like those electronic green highway signs. Wait, and the next word will appear. They come like rain. I stand like a tulip, a night cup, as they pour over me. They shower down, some lighting up like fireflies, slow enough to catch in cupped hands."

Another morning I woke up with the words "I'm a poet in my sleep." Eyes open, I added, "Awake I'm dull," only a slight exaggeration. I realized there was more to come and I dipped back into near sleep for the next provocative, slightly surreal image, "Asleep I seek your mouth, where lips are lounging like tanned tourists, legs slightly parted." Then, more awake, I wrote another line, "Awake I play ping pong." I continued this, drifting in and out of half-sleep, until I'd written the poem "Awake, Asleep."

I thought the poem was about me and my husband, but he told me he thought it was about me and myself. Now I think he's right.

I'm a poet in my sleep,
awake I'm dull.
Asleep I seek your mouth
where lips are lounging
like tanned tourists, legs slightly parted.
Awake I play ping pong.
Asleep I wander deserts in gauze gowns.
Awake I smile politely.
Asleep I dive to the bottom
where the fish arrange their bodies
in an ocean alphabet
and I can read their scales

like an ancient code explaining the mouths
of rivers and the ears of palms,
why day and night and wet and dry
and you and I exist.

At night in sleep you take me in,
By day I'm caught in shallows and left out.
Awake I talk
asleep I sing.
I'm the tide following the moon.
Awake you don't see me.
Asleep I'm your blood.
Red I course inside you,
rush right through your heart.
Awake words are heavy as pillars of salt.
Asleep I swim new ones with each stroke of my arm.
I'm so beautiful I'd never recognize myself.
No wonder I feel dread on the low threshold of dawn,
slipping into my heavy shoes
and leaving you again.

"Awake, Asleep" rose up because one part of me needed to communicate with another part of me.

Writing this way seems like being visited. And as with any visitor, I have to make room and time. Poet Robinson Jeffers wrote that no one "can make an invention or a poem by willing it. They come or they do not come. We can only prepare the way a little—sweep out distractions."

We have to dust, wash sheets, make sure there's an empty room, a bed, or at least a notebook on the night table, along with a flashlight. We have to make the invitation or allow an unexpected visitor to join us. We have to be quiet and listen for the bell or a knock. And we have to open the door.

PRACTICE

Keep a notebook or your journal by your bed. Early one morning write an awake/asleep poem. Catch some words from the unconscious dream world before they fade. Write them down. Then write a more awake line or two.

Awake I
Asleep I
Awake . . .

Ask your mind to drop in and out of dream. Try this with the words

On the inside, I'm . . .
On the outside, . . .

Don't worry if you don't end up with a poem. See these words as messages from a deep part of you to yourself. Some of your best poems *will* come from this place.

Before going to sleep now and then state a problem or topic to your unconscious and see what happens.

54

the blue socks

One summer in Chicago my younger brother, John, made fun of our dad, Julian, about the tacky, blue socks he was wearing. They were sky blue nylon with two black stripes around the top. "That's what started the whole thing," John says. "The socks were *so ugly.*"

When John got back to college in California he opened his suitcase and there were the thin, blue socks nestled in his shirts. On his next visit to Chicago *he* hid the socks somewhere in my parents' house. And now, nearly twenty-five years later, John and my parents are still wordlessly exchanging the blue socks.

Once my parents mailed the socks in a blue roll to John's neighbors in graduate student housing. A perplexed student delivered the pair to John's door. John jammed a sock in the bottom of a pencil mug in Chicago, thinking the folks would never find it. Soon enough the socks were both back in John's hands. My mother, Ethel, had sewed them onto a blue-and-black needlepoint of Escher birds and sent it as a birthday gift.

On a visit to John's house, Julian wore the socks and had to prop his legs on the coffee table to display those skinny blue nylon things with a black stripe. No one mentioned the socks.

Once during a family gathering, when Ethel and Julian were staying in Turlock, Julian got a message from the motel office to read a passage in the Gideon Bible. When he opened the Bible "there was a frigging blue sock," Julian says, "I'm apt to find one *anywhere.*" At John and Mary's wedding the blue sock flapped beside a rubber chicken hanging from the back of their Ford Pinto, "Sam."

Yesterday morning Julian left the hospital after a short stay. On the way home he thought his weakened left foot must be terribly swollen because his shoe didn't fit and he could hardly walk. When Julian got home and took off his shoe, he found a blue sock crammed in the toe.

Most socks, like most poems, stay in a drawer. But poems, like the blue socks that show up in unexpected places, are meant to be connectors. Not only do poems I write often connect me with another part of myself, they're meant to make a connection to a reader or listener. Poet Robert Bly insists a poem isn't a poem until it's read aloud and heard or received by someone.

Like the blue sock, a poem creates an exchange that brings people closer together. It can be a gift or a surprise for the reader. It can be a shock, unexpected and often unacknowledged. John and my parents never talk about the blue socks. "That's the beauty of it," Julian insists.

Emily Dickinson wrote, "This is my letter to the world, / that never wrote to me . . ." In a sense, a poem, like each hidden sock, is a love letter, even if we don't know to whom we're sending it, if it will arrive or if anyone will receive it.

55

bending light

It's winter solstice midnight in Chicago. There will be a little more sun each day now, as if the light that's been fading is bending back to us. My kids and I have just arrived from California. We're talking to my mom and dad in the small, front den walled with books where we always cram ourselves together, ignoring the rest of the large, brick house.

My father has leukemia, which is slowly taking his body. I'm still inspired by his manic flights of fancy. He's been singing the old thirties song "Avalon," with a twinkle, and remembering the Lockheed Vega, a vintage plane he photographed in the thirties. He's full of stories and bits of information he tells with humor and delight when he's not silent or angry.

Professor Starr, my father's telling us, an astronomer at the University of Chicago in the late 1800s, is rumored to have graded student papers by flinging them up a flight of stairs and assigning A's to the pages nearest the top. Starr created a different heaven in that fling, a constellation of papers by students he couldn't begin to assess, an arbitrary ranking bringing a new order like coyote creating chaos in the stars.

If only I could, like Professor Starr, create new rules, mess with the heavens and restore my father's body. A scientist, he's been driving us nuts taking his low temperature every half hour for over a year as if charting his body's thermal vagaries could give him some control over its processes run amok, with red and white blood cells on a slow boat to the ocean where all colors dissolve.

My father just washed his silver hair and it's combed straight back the way he's always combed it, the way his mother, Nanny, combed hers. He used to wear a nylon stocking cap like a beanie to control his hair after he washed it. But today it's a bit flyaway over bushy brows and black eyes with a ring of grey in the outer iris.

I want my children to hear everything my father says, his jokes in different accents, his off-color limericks and zany anecdotes reaching back into the rich Jewish family life in Chicago in the twenties and thirties.

How can my father be captured and held, how can I stave off the upcoming loss but in the possibility of a poem? It helps me to think I'll write my father's poem, a manic, leaping, angry poem with a pipeline of love into the earth's core. In a poem I can have him whole, bridging the world of the Russian rabbi, the geologist, the comedian and the naturalist loving and naming each landform.

Tolstoy says the role of the artist is not to find solutions but to "compel us to love life in all its countless, inexhaustible manifestations." That's what my father does and it's what my poem must do if I can ever write this love poem to him, whose passion for old airplanes, jokes, jazz, bicycles, woodpiles, paintings, photos, pre-Columbian art, feldspars, dolomite, calcite, aragonite, muskie, lake water, wildflowers, daffodils, the shadblow tree, grandchildren, my mother, each chickadee near his window in the Indiana dunes, whose passion compels *me* to love life.

My father's talking to my son, Daniel, now, about the earth's lower mantle and upper core, describing clues about their composition. Now they're talking about two types of quartz with right-handed and left-handed spirals, spiraling up and spiraling down. "We can only tell these types of quartz apart optically," Julian explains. "One bends the plane of polarized light one way, one bends it another way."

I need to make this poem to my father spiral up, spiral down, catch him and compel me, without him, to love life. I need to make a poem tipping on its axis that will somehow save him, through the coming of an inner solstice, through spiraling love, bending light.

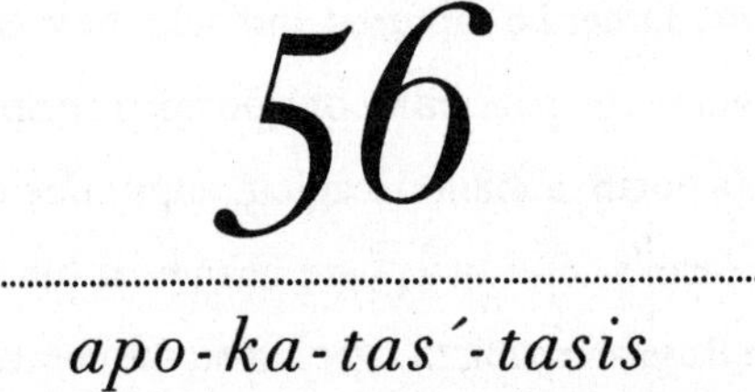

56

apo-ka-tas´-tasis

When I was twenty, misplaced in college in New York City, my boyfriend was being shipped to Vietnam. My mind and body staged a halt so complete that who I thought I was and would be was undone forever. Our culture has no name for this process—the unraveling of all the yarn in a sweater to undo a faulty stitch before we resume knitting, or digging back in an argument to uncover the pothole so we can re-create a foundation. I guess one name is *breakdown,* but there's no light in that word, no hope or possibility of renewal. And that winter in New York and back in Chicago I was unconsciously unraveling myself back to a new place of departure.

Sometimes, if things aren't going to fall apart, we have to take them apart. This may be what's heaped in a closet or it may be the way we've been living our lives.

Our culture doesn't see the value of this occurrence. When crisis or collapse is happening, it's almost impossible to recognize the unraveling, much less to honor it. It can feel like being bumped backwards out of control downhill into chaos as we level the old to break out of what binds us and create something new and free. If we had a name for this process, maybe we could see it differently and recognize the forward motion despite all appearances.

Belgian physicist Ilya Prigogine won a Nobel Prize in 1977 for his theory of dissipative structures, a kind of chaos theory. He showed that a period of dissolution is necessary before any system—a cell, society, solar system or person—can jump to a higher level of organization. Seen this way, unraveling or disintegration is a vital, creative event making room for the new.

The Hebrew Kabbalists wrote about this idea centuries earlier. They believed that to change from one reality to another a thing first must turn into nothing, where it reaches "the rung of nothingness," the state before creation when the egg has disappeared but the chick hasn't formed. *Chaos.* A worshipper, Kabbalists hold, "becomes like an empty tree, a flute played by God."

Such emptiness may be the state of being in which we can write poems that connect us with the most hidden parts of our hearts and psyches. In a poem, Roethke wrote, I can "shake the secrets from my deepest bones." We can begin to find words to describe and shape any "undoing" we may be experiencing. Words can help us express and possibly understand the unraveling. They can help us let go.

Whenever I see what seems like a disaster coming on, it helps me to say *apokatas´tasis* (apo-ka-tas´-tasis), from the Greek, meaning to set up again, to restore. It's an invocation, referring to good fortune hidden in apparent misfortune or tragedy. The word asks: out of apparent catastrophe, bring *blessing.* As soon as I can remember to say *apokatas´tasis* I realize I'll live through whatever bumping backwards I'm going through and I'll come out in a better place.

Rumi closed his poem "The New Rule,"

> The bowl breaks. Everywhere is falling everywhere.
> Nothing else to do.
>
> Here's the new rule: Break the wineglass,
> and fall toward the glassblower's breath.

Poems often slip into us in the realm where everything has fallen apart and can begin to come back together—in a crack between worlds, outside of time, in the realm of chaos.

PRACTICE

In her book *Centering,* M. C. Richards writes, "The way to center is by abandonment. Am I willing to give up what I have in order to be what I'm not yet?"

Many things need undoing. Sometimes our whole way of seeing who we are and talking about ourselves needs to come under the unraveling gaze of coyote.

Your job, your marriage, where you're living, a relationship with a child, friend or parent may need unraveling. Perhaps only your refrigerator needs defrosting and it's enough to toss most of the contents in the compost.

Make up your own name for this phenomenon. Naming it may help make this undoing less frightening.

When you break something or lose something or someone, don't weep, try celebrating the undoing. If you want, break a wineglass. Use words to set unraveling in motion,

out with
unwind
let loose
open, drop
dissolve
reveal
uncover

Remember the term *apokatas ´tasis.* Say it to yourself and even out loud when everything seems to be falling apart.

57

catching myself

I can't stand to lose anything. That's part of what all this writing is about for me. I create a container around me so I won't lose myself. I won't just evaporate into the universe unannounced or undefined. I write to catch myself. Me. Who is me?

I'm a row of little black books filled with tiny writing. I'm pasted-in pictures, scribbles, drawings and poems.

It's hard for me to see myself. When I put words on paper, in poems, in journals, there's evidence I exist. Here's my beauty, my vanity, fear, joy, loneliness. Me. If I put words in poems, I can begin to see my value. A mirror shows me my face, a poem shows me my soul.

In Chico's Upper Bidwell Park my friend Tanha and I began talking about the black caterpillars missing from the Dutchman's-pipe this year. I told her I need to write about this to capture the caterpillars. It's your way of making contact with them, Tanha says. She's noticed I almost think I don't *exist* if I'm not expressing. It's amazing that what's elusive to me is obvious to my friends. And I've often thought it would be nice to just *be,* and let go of my obsessive recording. But then I'd never have kept my journals or written my poems.

After we walked awhile along the Yahi trail amid wild grapes, mugwort and poison oak, we found a clump of Dutchman's-pipe with lots of black caterpillars munching. They're here this year after all, hooray!

I'm grateful I have the impulse to munch Dutchman's-pipe like the caterpillars and enter a cocoon where I can conjure poems and court metamorphosis. Maybe one day I'll grow powdery wings and graduate to silence.

For now, not only do I discover I exist when I write poems, I learn I'm larger than I thought. I extend up to where the air gets thin and down into the earth's core near the red hot spots. I sometimes sense, as Emily Dickinson wrote, that my "brain is wider than the sky." Where I end and where I begin, the boundaries of who I see myself to be, disappear when I'm writing poems.

58

caterpillar poets

For years when I've seen caterpillars heading away from the Dutchman's-pipe in Bidwell Park I've thought they were wandering to their death on the dusty path or road. Sometimes I've moved them back to the green pipe vines. Now I see that was a mistake.

When I walked in the park with Patricia recently, I was happy to see black caterpillars everywhere, some eating, some perched on foxtail and many traveling somewhere in a hurry. On the ridge where she lives, Patricia says, several caterpillars went "charging" toward her house not long ago. She watched them climb the rafters and suspend themselves by their heads from a thread. It was Patricia who noticed the caterpillars under the freeway.

With trucks rumbling overhead on Highway 99, walking on dirt never touched by rain, Patricia pointed out that the huge cement pillars supporting the freeway were covered with caterpillars. They seemed to be lifeless and disturbingly dusty. Some were attached by strands to the pillars, one or two still nodding from the effort.

Soon we noticed green-and-brown spiky chrysalises veined like leaves and arching like acrobats among the caterpillars. A few were empty. Like scenes from a surreal horror movie with a dramatic sound track, some of the caterpillars appeared to be growing spikes resembling small stalagmites and others had prickly green or brown husks arching out of their backs. They seemed to be little statues, hardening in front of our eyes, becoming armored cocoons in spite of themselves. Later I saw that their black caterpillar skin splits off and dangles below like old pantyhose.

That evening when I brought my family we found one chrysalis wiggling with something considering coming out. Unlike more advanced creatures—we humans with free will—I realize these creatures have no choice but to change.

My father's cousin Sylvia once challenged biologists she knows to find a term to describe a shift or transition changing someone or something from the inside out forever. Eventually one of the biologists phoned her with the word *instar*. The dictionary defines *instar* first, "to stud with, or as if with stars." And next, as "an insect or other arthropod between molts, as during metamorphosis."

Instar is the word for an organism (an insect, mind you, like a pipevine swallowtail) in the state of radical change. We have no term for such change in humans. Maybe our culture doesn't recognize that such change is possible. Maybe we need to expand the meaning of *instar* or come up with a term just for us two-leggeds.

One reason to write poems, I think, is to capture moments of awareness that lead to a shift. Writing poems may help us see and even create this change. Often embedded in a poem is a moment of perception describing such a shift, when suddenly the world looks different, when we're at a watershed rolling toward a warmer or perhaps an icier ocean. We may feel like we're emerging from a cocoon.

Since my walk with Patricia I've stopped moving caterpillars from the path unless, maybe, they're on a busy road in the blazing sun. The caterpillars need to be left alone to search for the hard, safe spot their instincts are seeking. There they can split, surrender and transform into slender creatures with dazzling blue wingtips, pipevine swallowtails that feed on my false lilac.

Who knows where I'm going and what I may become if I trust my intuition. In poems we make a blind charge into ourselves and hope what emerges has wings. We need all of ourselves to fly, the right and left, high and low, dark and light of ourselves. Caterpillars need the rigid structure of the chrysalis to undergo metamorphosis. They follow their instincts, but the timing must be right and the steps must be taken or they won't be in the right spot when they shed their skin.

Sometimes it's best if we don't know where we're going as long as we take the steps. We follow instinct and intuition no matter how dusty or dry the path. We may find answers suspended by a thread in a dry, desolate area. Caterpillar poets, we need to wander until we find the right spot.

PRACTICE

Think of a time when an irreversible change took place in your life. It may not be a change that was visible to anyone but you. It may have been a shift in the way you experience the world or your parents or your children.

It may be the first time you fell in or out of love. It may have to do with a death of someone close, or a birth. It may be a shift in your idea of who you are.

What's a shift or change that's taking place in your life right now? Compare this shift to something in nature. Compare it to something in the life of a specific tree, plant or animal.

List shifts you've experienced in your life. Times of opening or closing, or stunning realization. Write them down. They may want to be described in a poem.

59

a seng song pot of possibilities

Today on the way to our roasted eggplant with provolone and watercress yuppie lunch, my friend Jane and I drove past a chain link fence. It was guarding a stretch of newly turned black dirt where a Chinese woman was on her knees planting flowers. A few feet to her left, concentrating intently on the spade in his hands, was her young black-haired son. Behind them we noticed rows of huge, glazed garden pots, green, blue and black. Jane pulled over and we decided to get out. I chose a green pot, one of the smaller ones and still nearly two feet across, crackly and with areas streaked black.

I wrote a twenty-dollar check to Seng Song Pottery, admiring even the pot's flaws, including a small triangle of concrete glazed onto its side. We hauled the pot with muddy water rolling in the bottom onto the back seat of Jane's car and went to lunch.

Now as I drive past rolling, grey hills toward home, just out of sight of the bay, 3:42 P.M. on I-80 by Lagoon Valley and Peña Adobe Roads near Vacaville, the pot sits empty, full of possibility, waiting to be filled with a small lemon tree, or heather, or clumps of lilies and ranunculus or even kindling and firewood if I place it by the fireplace in the house. Maybe I won't put *anything* in it. What I think attracted me most to these huge pots was their dark, open emptiness, waiting to receive something.

Now my green pot is propped just behind my seat. I can reach back and feel the cool glaze gritty from the nursery as I bring it home, a seng song pot of possibilities, like a poem—empty and full as I am.

the poem bridge

Two boys bob underwater and pop up with a brown bottle at One Mile pool. They're talking about the rocks and dirt they've poured out. "Now it can be a water container," one boy says, holding the empty bottle upside down.

Below the bridge a yellow twig jackknives over the falls and disappears in bubbles. Here comes Rabbi Fisdel with a big smile and a small group celebrating the Jewish New Year. It's the new moon close to the autumnal equinox. We've gathered at the bridge to recall the year in a ceremony called Tashlich, which means "to cast out." It's rewarding to look back, see where we've run amok and give ourselves a chance to start fresh.

The rabbi sports a tan safari hat over a round face, curly red hair and beard. The people on the bridge act like they've never seen a fish, pointing and pulling their kids over to see. Trout swim into the shadow of a large sycamore leaf curled like a bird with raised wings, or an angel.

"On Tashlich," the rabbi explains, "we drop bread in the water to symbolize letting go of sins." Nancy says, "The fish are going to swallow our sins!" Laughing, the rabbi remarks, "Better them than us!" The two boys with the bottle appear under the bridge. We peer down and the kids scramble back to the pool across the dam. The sycamore leaf bumps against the creekside rocks and blackberry vines. A couple crosses the bridge and the man asks, "Anyone have change for a dollar?"

We lean over the railing with our bread as the rabbi describes sins as a complex of mistakes that become a wall blocking feeling and communication with the Almighty. He suggests we see the bread as that wall. I clutch a thick chunk of whole-wheat from Chico Breadworks, nearly half a loaf.

The rabbi, in his Crocodile Dundee hat, says "Let's cast our sins to the sea." He invokes an ancient blessing as we fling mistakes and watch bits of bread ignite concentric circles of light and shadow over darting fish in the water. He chants "lo lo lo lo lo lo lo . . ." as I breathe creek air and intone, "I cast out my fear, my doubt, my fullness with myself. . . ." The adults whisper the way I do while kids bombard the fish.

Later I sit below the bridge with my feet in the creek and the sun on my back. Reflected light flickers on the bridge's concave belly.

A bridge between this and that, my side and yours, light and dark, past and future, what we can see and what we can't. A bridge like the new year when, it is said, the ancient gates are open between this year and the next, between who we've been and who we want to be. Students of the Kabbalah sing a folk song with the words, "All the world is just a narrow bridge. And above all is not to fear, not to fear at all."

A child and her mother amble across the span barefoot. They pause to look down and listen to the falls. The mother carries four black shoes, two large and two small, with laces dangling. Across the bridge a young man lobs his red ball to a friend.

People stop in the middle, suspended, listen and look down into the creek. A man in a pink shirt with a blond toddler gestures toward the water, like all the mothers and fathers. "See the fish?" he asks.

It's alive, this bridge, with the possibility of fish poem, bread-in-the-water poem, red-football poem, casting-out-mistakes poem, tiny see-through-fly poem, brown-bottle-emptying-and-filling poem, damsel fly, woodpecker, acorn, oak, creek-rushing-to-the-ocean poem.

The last of our bread floats above quiet fish as I put on my shoes and walk home from the bridge.

The author has made every effort to trace the ownership of all copyrighted materials in this volume. If there are any errors or omissions, corrections will gladly be made in future editions. Thanks are due to the following authors and publishers.

Francisco Alarcón, "A poem" and "A poet is a river," copyright © 1992 by Francisco X. Alarcón. Reprinted by permission of the author.

Phoebe Ambrosia, "I am not one of these," reprinted by permission of the author.

Anonymous Navajo poem from *Navajo Code Talkers* by Doris A. Paul, Dorrance Pub. Co. Inc., Pittsburgh, 1973.

Cassandra Sagan Bell, "Back to Arcadia," *Waiting to Move the Mountain,* CPITS 1994 statewide anthology. Reprinted by permission of the author.

Lucille Clifton, "i come to read them poems," copyright © 1987 by Lucille Clifton. Reprinted from *Next: New Poems,* by Lucille Clifton, with the permission of BOA Editions, Ltd., 92 Park Ave., Brockport, NY 14420.

Jessica Constant, "Three Dreams," reprinted by permission of the author.

e. e. cummings, "love is more thicker than forget," copyright 1939, © 1967, 1991 by the Trustees for the e. e. cummings Trust, from *Complete Poems: 1904–1962,* by e. e. cummings, edited by George J. Firmage. Reprinted by permission of Liveright Publishing Corporation.

Holly Dugas, excerpt from "I come from," reprinted by permission of the author.

Ellen Galena, excerpt from "Shine Bright," reprinted by permission of the author.

Jack Grapes, excerpt from "I Like My Own Poems Best," from *Trees, Coffee, and the Eyes of Deer* by Jack Grapes. Bombshelter Press, 1987, 1995, L.A. Reprinted by permission of the author.

Erica Castillo Henderson, "Wish Dome," reprinted by permission of the author.

Vicente Huidobro, "Altazor" (9 lines) from *The Selected Poems of Vicente Huidobro*. Copyright © 1963 by Empreza Editora Zig Zag, S.A., © 1981 by David Guss. Reprinted by permission of New Directions Publishing Corp.

Galway Kinnell, excerpt from "The Poem," from *Body Rags* by Galway Kinnell. Copyright © 1965, 1966, 1967 by Galway Kinnell. Reprinted by permission of Houghton Mifflin Co. All rights reserved.

Denise Levertov, "Writing in the Dark" from *Candles in Babylon*. Copyright © 1982 by Denise Levertov. Reprinted by permission of New Directions Publishing Corp.

Marianne Moore, "O to Be a Dragon," copyright © 1957 by Marianne Moore, renewed 1985 by Lawrence E. Brinn and Louise Crane, Executors of the Estate of Marianne Moore, from *The Complete Poems of Marianne Moore*. Used by permission of Viking Penguin, a division of Penguin Books USA Inc.

Pablo Neruda, excerpt from "Poetry," from *The Selected Poems of Pablo Neruda*, edited by Nathaniel Tarn, copyright © 1973. Reprinted by permission of Jonathan Cape Random House, UK, London.

Pablo Neruda, from *Odes to Common Things* by Pablo Neruda. Selected and illustrated by Ferris Cook. Odes (Spanish) copyright © 1994 by Pablo Neruda and Fundacion Pablo Neruda. Odes (English translation) copyright © 1994 by Ken Krabbencroft. By permission of Little Brown and Co.

Howard Norman, translator, "All the warm nights/sleep in moonlight" and excerpts from "There was a storm once" by Jacob Nibengenesabe in *The Wishing Bone Cycle: Narrative Poems from the Swampy Cree Indians*. Ross-Erikson Publishing, Santa Barbara, 1972, 1982.

Rumi, excerpt from "The New Rule" and from "An Egypt That Doesn't Exist" from *Open Secret*. Reprinted by permission of Threshold Books, RD 4, Box 600, Putney, VT 05346.

Charles Simic, "Emily Dickinson," from *Dime-Store Alchemy: The Art of Joseph Cornell by Charles Simic*. Copyright © 1992 by Charles Simic. First published by The Ecco Press in 1992. Reprinted by permission.

Siyaki, reprinted from *The Sky Clears* by A. Grove Day by permission of the University of Nebraska Press. Copyright © 1951 by A. Grove Day.

Richard Wilbur, "Apology," from *Things of This World*, copyright © 1956 and renewed 1984 by Richard Wilbur, reprinted by permission of Harcourt Brace & Company.

W. B. Yeats, excerpt from "The Lake Isle of Innisfree." Reprinted with the permission of Simon & Schuster from *The Poems of W.B. Yeats, A New Edition*, edited by Richard J. Finneran (New York: Macmillan, 1983).